South Carolina

Always In Season

A Recipe Collection

by

Ann Burger

McClanahan
Publishing House

International Standard Book Number 0-913383 85-6
Library of Congress Card Catalog Number 2002103891

Cover design and book layout by James Asher Graphics
Cover illustration by James Asher
Back cover photo by Wade Spees
Photographs other than family are courtesy of *The Post and Courier*

Manufactured in the United States of America

All book order correspondence should be addressed to:

McClanahan Publishing House, Inc.
P. O. Box 100
Kuttawa, KY 42055

1-800-544-6959

www.kybooks.com
books@kybooks.com

Dedicated to my parents,
Edith and Jack Mitchell

Foreword

This cookbook owes everything to family and friends, old and new. It's a personal book, mostly seasonal recipes for the best of what South Carolina has to offer from land, sea and air. But there are also recipes here that have little to do with the Palmetto State – other than that they're just plain good. We do like to eat around here, you know.

I didn't set quotas for particular kinds of recipes, or for a particular number of recipes per season. If it's a dish we like, then into the book it went. I attributed recipes to their sources to the best of my ability and memory, as far back as the family could recall.

Many thanks are due to the many people who contributed to this book.

My husband, Ken, provided me with much more than his beautiful essays on the seasons. He happily offered kitchen help, moral support, and a willingness to eat any dish I was tinkering with (several times). He encouraged me, and he has always been there to make me believe that I can do anything, because for some reason he believes that himself.

My wonderful mother, Edith Mitchell, worked as hard on this project as I did, and it is truly as much her book as mine – in some ways, more. She spent many long hours, many days, carefully measuring out ingredients for dishes that she usually makes by instinct, and that isn't as easy as it sounds. She will always be my best teacher.

Jack Mitchell, my father, has always provided us plenty of terrific material to work with – venison, ducks, doves, fish, shrimp, and more, all caught by his own hand. I was never a hunter, or much of a fisherman either, but hopefully I'll always be able to do what Mom has done: Cook what he brings home in a loving, satisfying way.

Edie Blair, my sister, is the cook I'm always trying to keep up with. Almost every time we talk, she's got a new recipe to tell me about – and there hasn't yet been one that I didn't want to try myself. She inspires and supports me in every way, and you'll see lots of her recipes in this book.

My aunt, Jean Mitchell, is our shrimp and crab expert. Her dock on the waterfront in Mount Pleasant was the setting for many a glorious catch, and she's one of those wise cooks who know that when you've got a great foundation like fresh-caught local seafood, the last thing you should do is throw a lot of extra flavors at it.

A hearty thank-you goes also to all the family friends who have shared their best recipes with us over the years. You have made our lives more delicious.

I'm grateful to *The Post and Courier* — particularly publisher Larry Tarleton, former features editor Betsy Cantler and my current boss, Steve Mullins — for giving a good ol' home cook with no formal culinary training a chance to be the food editor. It's been a pleasure. And I raise a flute of the finest Champagne to the paper's wine columnist, Andy Felts, who provided me with his patient computer assistance when time came for me to assemble the scattered pieces of this project.

I appreciate also the support and confidence of Paula Cunningham from McClanahan Publishing.

Finally, lest I forget, here's a little chin scratch for Shelley the Wonder Cat, who is very good company and knows just what to do to help me keep everything in perspective.

I hope you enjoy "South Carolina: Always in Season." Happy cooking!

Ann Burger

Table of Contents

Spring

We were lucky in the South because spring came rushing to us as if she were looking for someone to announce her early arrival. And we were always more than happy to oblige.

For me and other little boys who had been swaddled in sweaters for the long winter, the first smells of freedom came when we burst from the house in short sleeves and ran like wild ponies down into the nearby fields. There the fresh green stalks of wild onions announced their presence with a pungent aroma of new growth.

In dungarees, sneakers and T-shirts we would frolic through fields ablaze with the red-topped tassels of sour grass, pulling the stalks through our teeth to extract its tart juices. And there we could lie back, feeling the still-cold earth beneath us while gazing at the swirls of clouds up above.

Sometimes the cumulus concoctions reminded me of meringue piled high atop one of my mother's lemon pies. Others resembled coconut flakes distributed haphazardly around one of her tall, delicious cakes.

These were precious days to be savored like sweet tea before the blowtorch of summer ignited the skillet we lived in. These were days when azaleas bloomed like trumpets announcing the seasonal change. When the doors and windows were opened and asparagus and strawberries were piled on the kitchen counters. When insects buzzed about the shrubbery, screen porches were swept out and a layer of pollen was wiped off the lawn chairs with a wet cloth.

From March to May we pretended to pay attention to our teachers in class, but we could not ignore the warming breezes that called to us just outside the classroom window.

With the promise of an endless summer hanging like salted hams in the smokehouse, just out of reach, yet close enough to taste, we hungered for that freedom. Which, like most delightful things in life, is even better than the consumption itself.

Ken Burns

Boursin

2 (8-ounce) packages cream cheese, softened
¼ cup mayonnaise
2 teaspoons Dijon mustard
2 tablespoons finely-chopped fresh chives
2 tablespoons finely-chopped fresh dill
1 clove garlic, very finely minced
Salt and pepper to taste

In a mixing bowl, blend all the ingredients with an electric mixer until smooth and well-blended. Refrigerate until well chilled. Makes enough to serve about 8 as a dip or spread.

Boursin is great for parties because you can make it up to four days ahead of time. In fact, I think it gets better day by day.

Boursin is a rich, garlic-and-herb cheese that's perfect for spreading on crackers or scooping up on raw vegetables – carrot sticks, celery sticks, strips of bell pepper, anything you like. My mother, Edith Mitchell, decided years ago that she could come up with a homemade version of this "gourmet" cheese — and here's the result. The fresh chives and dill make it a springtime favorite.

Don't miss the recipe for Butterflies with Spinach and Boursin later in this chapter. It puts this spread, usually an appetizer, to work deliciously in a main dish.

Sea Island Strawberry Bread

*S*trawberries are the first fruit to come into season in the Lowcountry. When the "u-pick" farms on the Sea Islands open in mid - to late April, we flock out to the fields with everybody else to get our first taste of spring. This delicious — and deliciously simple — bread is a specialty of my sister, Edie Blair. Her old friend Rob Robinson, who now lives in Asheville, N.C., gave her the recipe years ago, and now it's as much a family tradition as berry-pickin' is.

2 cups sliced fresh strawberries
2 cups sugar (plus extra for sprinkling)
3 cups plus 2 tablespoons all-purpose flour
1 tablespoon cinnamon
1 teaspoon salt
1 teaspoon baking soda
1¼ cups canola oil
4 large eggs, beaten
1¼ cups chopped pecans

Preheat the oven to 350 degrees. Grease and flour two 9x5-inch loaf pans. Place the strawberries in a bowl; sprinkle with a little sugar and set aside (to draw out juices). In another bowl, combine the 2 cups of sugar with the flour, cinnamon, salt and baking soda. Mix well. Combine the oil and eggs with the strawberries, then stir them into the flour mixture. Add the pecans and stir until the dry ingredients are just moistened. Divide the batter between the prepared pans and bake for 45-50 minutes. Let the bread cool completely in the pans on a wire rack. Makes two loaves, about 8-10 slices per loaf.

Mrs. Peery's Orange Muffins

2 large eggs
½ cup freshly-squeezed orange juice
¼ cup sugar
2 tablespoons vegetable oil
2 cups buttermilk biscuit mix
½ cup orange marmalade

Preheat oven to 400 degrees. Combine the eggs, orange juice, sugar and oil in a bowl; beat well with an electric mixer. Add the biscuit mix and beat for 30 seconds. Stir in the marmalade. Spray 12 standard muffin cups lightly with nonstick cooking spray. Spoon the batter into the cups, filling each three-quarters full. Bake for 15 minutes, or until the tops are golden brown. Makes 12 muffins.

These easy muffins are a great complement for a spring salad, rounding it out into a light lunch or dinner. The Mrs. Peery of the title is Lidie Peery, the mother of family friend Lisa Peery. Lisa was like a part of our family when she and my sister Edie shared an apartment after college.

Baked Brie with Chives

*A*t all those spring wedding showers and graduation get-togethers, creamy rounds of Brie cheese baked in a golden pastry crust make beautiful additions to the table.

For a duo of savory and sweet, offer one wheel of Brie with chives and another wheel of Brown Sugar Baked Brie.

Pastry dough for a single-crust, 9-inch pie
1 (8-ounce) wheel of Brie cheese, chilled
1 large egg, beaten with 1 tablespoon water
1-1½ tablespoons snipped fresh chives

Preheat the oven to 400 degrees. Roll out the pastry dough so that it's about ⅛-inch thick. Cut out two circles – one 7 inches in diameter and one 3 inches in diameter. Place the wheel of Brie in the middle of the larger circle and fold the pastry up, wrapping the cheese and pleating the pastry up snugly over the sides and the rim of the cheese. Brush the bit of pastry that's on top with a little of the beaten egg. Sprinkle the chives evenly over the exposed cheese. Place the small circle of pastry on top of the cheese, pressing down at the edges to seal the cheese completely inside. Brush the top of the pastry with some of the egg. If you wish, make small decorative cutouts from the remaining scraps of dough and arrange them on top of the pastry, brushing with the egg. Place the pastry-wrapped cheese on a baking sheet and bake for about 20 minutes, until the pastry is golden and crisp. Remove the pan from the oven, place it on a wire rack, and let the cheese cool for 15 minutes. To serve, place the pastry on a serving plate and slice it into wedges. Makes 4-6 appetizer servings.

Brown Sugar Baked Brie

¾ cup chopped pecans
3 tablespoons light brown sugar
¼ cup Kahlúa or other coffee-flavored liqueur
1 (14 ounce) wheel of Brie cheese,
thoroughly chilled

I've seen this served with apple slices, plain crackers and even gingersnaps. However you serve it, be sure you don't overbake the Brie; it should be soft, but not so melted that it won't hold its shape on a cracker or wedge of fruit.

Place the pecans in a microwave-safe bowl and microwave on high for 4-6 minutes, stirring every 2 minutes. Remove the pecans from the oven, stir in the brown sugar and Kahlúa, and set aside. Cut the rind from the top of the Brie, stopping about ½ inch from the edge (cut as closely to the top as you can so you don't waste the cheese); discard the rind. Place the Brie on a microwave-safe plate and spoon the pecan mixture over the top. Microwave the cheese on high for 1½ - 2 minutes, or until it softens to a spreadable consistency without being runny. If your microwave doesn't have a carousel, turn the plate a half-turn after 45 seconds. Serve immediately with crackers, apple slices, etc. Makes 12-15 appetizer servings.

Mandarin Orange and Avocado Salad

ere's a neat, light salad we love. A touch of sugar and a dab of mayonnaise turn a packaged salad dressing mix into a terrific topping for oranges, avocadoes and a couple of kinds of lettuce.

1 envelope Italian salad dressing mix
2 teaspoons sugar
1 tablespoon mayonnaise
1 good-sized head Bibb lettuce
1 good-sized head romaine lettuce
5 green onions, finely chopped
2 (11-ounce) cans mandarin oranges, drained
2 ripe avocadoes, cut into chunks
½ cup sliced almonds, toasted

Prepare the salad dressing according to package directions, adding in the sugar and mayonnaise at the same time. Refrigerate and let chill thoroughly. Tear both kinds of lettuce into bite-size pieces and place them in a serving bowl. Toss in the onion with your hands or salad "fingers." Add the oranges and avocado and toss gently. Pour the chilled dressing on top and toss gently (use as much or as little dressing as you like; you might have some left over). Sprinkle the sliced almonds on top, then serve. Makes 6 generous servings.

This salad is very pretty if served on individual plates. Mix the lettuces and green onion together in a bowl, then place some on each salad plate. Arrange the oranges next. Cut the avocado into wedges, rather than chunks, and fan them out on one side of the plate, then drizzle the dressing on top. Sprinkle the almonds on last.

Warm Green Beans with Roasted Garlic/Mustard Vinaigrette

1 pound fresh small green beans
1 tablespoon salt
4 cloves garlic, unpeeled
½ cup plus 2 tablespoons extra virgin olive oil
1 tablespoon Dijon mustard
3 tablespoons red wine vinegar
1 tablespoon honey
Salt and freshly-ground pepper, to taste
1 tablespoon butter
2 tablespoons snipped fresh chives

Rinse the beans and snap off the ends if needed. Bring a large saucepan of water to a vigorous boil, then add the beans and the tablespoon of salt. Cook until the beans are just tender; drain immediately, then rinse in very cold water until the beans are cool, then drain again.

To make the vinaigrette, place the garlic cloves on a small baking sheet and drizzle them with 2 tablespoons of the olive oil. Bake the garlic in a 350-degree oven until the cloves are soft to the touch, about 30-40 minutes. Cool to room temperature, then squeeze the garlic cloves out of their papery jackets into a small mixing bowl. Using a fork, mash the garlic into a coarse purée. Add the mustard, vinegar, honey, and the salt

*Holly Herrick, the restaurant reviewer for **The Post and Courier**, is also a Cordon Bleu-trained chef who has quite a knack for developing recipes. She writes a monthly column for the paper's food section when the farmers' markets are open (April through October), and she always shares terrific recipes, such as this one.*

Use the very smallest, freshest green beans to make this wonderful side dish. It's tailor-made for those still-just-a-touch-cool nights that follow the earliest days of spring.

and pepper, to taste. Whisk well, then, while whisking constantly, drizzle in the remaining ½ cup olive oil very slowly. Set the vinaigrette aside at room temperature. To serve, heat a sauté pan over medium-high heat. Add the butter; when it melts, add the beans and sauté quickly, just to warm. Season, if needed, with salt and pepper. Remove the pan from the heat and toss the beans with the vinaigrette and the chives. Serve immediately. Makes 6 servings.

Copper Pennies

*lthough I love carrots now, I refused to eat them when I was a child. Thank goodness our tastes mature. I hate thinking of all the wonderful food I would have missed if my taste buds had closed for business when I was 10!*

This recipe is from the collection of my aunt, Jean Mitchell. The ground ginger combines with orange to make these carrots especially appealing.

1 pound peeled baby carrots
1 teaspoon sugar
1 teaspoon cornstarch
¼ teaspoon salt
¼ teaspoon ground ginger
¼ cup orange juice
1 tablespoon butter

In a saucepan, with salted water to cover, cook the carrots for 20 minutes, or until they're tender. Drain well. Combine the sugar, cornstarch, salt, ginger and orange juice in a small saucepan. Cook over low heat, stirring constantly, for about 5 minutes, or until the mixture thickens. Add the butter, stirring well to melt. Pour the sauce over the carrots and stir gently to coat well. Makes 3-4 servings.

Okra Soup

Vegetable oil
2 pounds lean stew beef
5 soup bones
1 (14½-ounce) can beef broth
4 cans water (use the broth can to measure)
2 pounds fresh okra
14 ounces canned crushed tomatoes
2 teaspoons sugar
Salt and freshly-ground black pepper, to taste
2 bay leaves

*P*alm Sundays when we were little always brought the okra soup lunch at church. Mom used to make pots and pots of soup for the parish event. Here's her recipe. Try this with cornbread for a terrific lunch.

Add a bit of vegetable oil to a soup pot – just enough to coat the bottom. Over medium-high heat, brown the meat and the soup bones. Add the beef broth and water, then reduce the heat to a simmer and cook for 1 hour. Remove stem ends and tips from the okra, then slice the okra into small rounds. Add the okra to the pot and simmer for 45 minutes. Add the tomatoes, sugar, salt, pepper and bay leaves, then simmer until the okra is completely tender. Remove the bay leaves before serving. Makes 6-8 servings.

Orange, Onion and Olive Salad

he Post and Courier's cookbook columnist, Marion Sullivan, has served as a consultant to some of the Lowcountry's top chefs as they translate their restaurant recipes into portions and methods that are approachable for people like you and me who cook in much smaller numbers. Marion has extensive catering experience and is an accomplished developer of recipes. I'm very grateful to her for sharing several of her recipes for this book.

3 tablespoons red wine vinegar
¼ cup extra-virgin olive oil
Salt and freshly-ground black pepper, to taste
1 clove garlic
4 navel oranges, peeled and sliced in rounds
1 small red onion, thinly sliced
2 tablespoons pitted, chopped Kalamata olives
1 large head Boston lettuce, leaves separated, washed, patted dry, and refrigerated in a plastic bag so they will crisp

Whisk together the vinegar and oil. Add salt and pepper to taste. Mash the garlic clove slightly to release its flavor and add it to the oil and vinegar. Layer the sliced oranges and onions in a glass or ceramic bowl. Pour the dressing over them, cover, and refrigerate for at least 3 hours, or overnight. When ready to serve, drain the oranges and onions, discarding the garlic, but reserving the dressing. Taste the dressing and, if needed, add more salt or pepper. Make 4 lettuce cups. Divide the oranges and onions between them, dot them with the olives, sprinkle with dressing if needed, and serve. Makes 4 servings.

"My college roommate, Betty Edge, taught me how to make this salad," Marion tells me. The trick is to check the dressing for salt and pepper after you marinate the oranges and onions, because the sweet juices from the oranges usually change the taste of the dressing. Kalamata olives are worth the bother of pitting; they add a great little pop of flavor.

Layered Spinach Salad

6 cups loosely-packed, torn spinach leaves
3 hard-boiled eggs, sliced into rounds
6 slices bacon, fried crisp, then crumbled
1 small bunch lettuce (your favorite kind), torn
1 medium red onion, sliced, separated into rings
1 (10-ounce) package frozen peas, thawed
2 cups mayonnaise
1 cup sour cream
1 cup grated Swiss cheese
Paprika, as a garnish, if desired

In a pretty serving bowl (about 2½ quarts), layer ingredients as follows: spinach, egg slices, bacon crumbles, lettuce, onion rings, peas. In a mixing bowl, stir together mayonnaise and sour cream. Spread on top of salad. Sprinkle cheese on top. Cover tightly and refrigerate to chill through. Sprinkle paprika on top before serving, if desired. Makes about 8 servings.

There are scads of layered-salad recipes out there, and they're justifiably popular — not just because they taste great, but because they're so easy to prepare ahead of time if you're entertaining. Fresh spinach from the farmers' market gives this salad a lift and sets it apart.

This is one of those "I can't remember where we got this, can you?" recipes from the family's voluminous files.

Never-Too-Much Zucchini Pie

*P*rolific zucchini plants are the bane of many home vegetable gardeners, but we never have that problem, thanks mostly to this recipe, which came from an ad in a women's magazine about 20 to 25 years ago. It originally called for minuscule amounts of dried herbs, but we use fresh herbs from the garden in flavorful, satisfying quantities.

This is a family lunch staple from spring right on through to fall. When local tomatoes start coming into the farmers' markets in the summer, we slice those up to serve alongside.

Feel free to be flexible with the fresh herbs in this dish. Start out with the amounts suggested and adjust to your taste from there.

4 cups thinly-sliced fresh zucchini
1 cup chopped onion
1 medium clove garlic, finely minced
4-6 tablespoons butter
¼ cup chopped fresh parsley
3 tablespoons chopped fresh basil
2 teaspoons chopped fresh oregano
Salt and freshly-ground black pepper, to taste
2 large eggs, beaten
8 ounces shredded mozzarella cheese
1 (8-ounce) can crescent dinner rolls
2 tablespoons Dijon mustard

Preheat the oven to 375 degrees. In a large skillet or pot set over medium-high heat, cook the zucchini, onions and garlic in the butter for 10 minutes, until the onions are lightly browned and the zucchini is softened. Stir in the parsley, basil, oregano, salt and pepper; cook 5 minutes more, then remove the pan from the heat. Combine the beaten eggs and mozzarella in a bowl, then stir them into the zucchini mixture. Separate the eight crescent rolls into triangles. Arrange them in the bottom and up the sides of an ungreased 10-inch pie plate; pinch the seams together to seal. Spread the mustard over the crust. Pour in the zucchini mixture. Bake the pie for 18-20 minutes; if necessary, cover the edges of the crust with foil to keep them from getting too brown. Remove the pie from the oven and let it stand 10 minutes before slicing. Makes 6 servings.

Lemon Chicken Salad with Grapes

½ cup mayonnaise
¼ cup sour cream
1 tablespoon sugar
½ teaspoon grated lemon peel
1 tablespoon fresh lemon juice
½ teaspoon ground ginger
¼ teaspoon salt, or to taste
2 cups cooked, cubed chicken
1 cup seedless green grape halves
1 cup thinly-sliced celery
½ cup slivered almonds
Lettuce leaves
Small clusters of grapes

Here's a great lunch idea for a spring day. It's been in our family files since I was young enough to turn up my nose at the whole idea of chicken with grapes. When I was finally persuaded to try it, I was won over in no time at all.

Stir together the mayonnaise, sour cream, sugar, lemon peel, lemon juice, ginger and salt. Add the chicken, grapes and celery; stir gently to coat with the dressing. Cover the salad and chill it for at least 2 hours before serving. When ready to serve, lightly toast the almonds just until they start to smell nutty (don't let them burn – watch closely). Serve the salad on lettuce leaves, topped with toasted almonds and small grape clusters alongside to garnish. Makes 4 servings.

Here's a neat serving idea: cut a cantaloupe in half and scoop out the pulp and seeds. Serve the salad in the cantaloupe.

Butterflies with Spinach and Boursin

Part of my job as food editor is looking over all the recipes and food-related stories that come to the newspaper each day via our wire services, such as The Associated Press. This is a recipe I saw on the wire a couple of years ago. I printed it out to take home and try, and we loved it.

Unfortunately, I didn't know then that I'd be writing this book, so I didn't record the source.

The tender little spinach I see each spring at our farmers' markets is ideal for this dish – the leaves are as sweet as can be. I've made a minor change or two in the recipe – including the use of my mother's homemade Boursin. The original recipe called for purchased Boursin, which works beautifully; I just happen to like Mom's better.

8 cups loosely-packed baby spinach leaves, stems removed
16 ounces butterfly pasta
2 tablespoons extra virgin olive oil
¾ cup homemade Boursin, or one 5.2-ounce container purchased
¼ to ½ cup cooking water from pasta
Salt and freshly-ground black pepper, to taste

Tear any large spinach leaves into smaller pieces. Place all the spinach in a colander; rinse briefly in cold water. Set aside. Bring a large pot of salted water to a boil; cook and drain the pasta according to package directions. While the pasta is cooking, heat the olive oil in a skillet over medium heat. When the oil is hot, add the spinach and cook just until the leaves are barely wilted, only a minute or two. Take the skillet off the heat, add the Boursin, and begin stirring it in to melt it. Place the skillet back over medium-low heat, continuing to stir until the cheese becomes creamy, with a sauce-like consistency. Save about ½ cup of the pasta-cooking water, then drain off the rest. Add the saved cooking water to the Boursin sauce and spinach, stirring to blend. Pour the sauce over the pasta and season with salt and pepper. Gently stir until the pasta is well coated. Makes 4 servings.

Penne Pasta with Asparagus and Caramelized Onions

¼ cup plus 4 tablespoons olive oil, divided
3 tablespoons butter
1 tablespoon light brown sugar
2 sweet onions (such as Vidalias), thinly sliced and separated into rings
1 pound fresh asparagus, woody ends snapped off
1 large clove garlic, minced
1 teaspoon kosher salt (or less, to taste)
¾ pound uncooked penne pasta
Freshly-grated Parmesan cheese

Place 4 tablespoons of the olive oil, the butter and the brown sugar in a large skillet over medium heat; when they begin to bubble, add the onions and stir gently to coat. Turn the heat to medium-low and cook for 20-30 minutes, until the onions are soft and golden brown; stir frequently to keep the onions from sticking to the pan. Meanwhile, slice the asparagus on the diagonal into 2-inch slices; place in a baking dish. Pour the remaining ¼ cup olive oil over the asparagus, and sprinkle the minced garlic and the salt over the top. Stir gently to coat the asparagus. Roast on the top rack of a 450-degree oven for 12-15 minutes, stirring once or twice during cooking time. Cook the pasta in boiling salted water, according to package directions, until it is slightly firm to the bite. Drain. Combine the pasta with the caramelized onions and the asparagus, stirring gently. Serve with Parmesan to pass at the table, as desired. Makes 4 servings.

*My sister, Edie Blair, is a creative, adventurous cook – and a wonderful cook as well. When the parents' association at her children's school, Porter-Gaud, decided to publish a cookbook, the members did just what I would have done: they asked Edie to head up the recipe-testing committee. The book, **Tested by Time: A Collection of Charleston Recipes** (Favorite Recipes Press, 1997) has been a great success.*

*This recipe is one of my favorites from the book. Asparagus is the first spring vegetable in the Lowcountry and I'm always happy to find recipes that let its sweet goodness shine through. Edie's friend Harriett Keith contributed it to **Tested by Time.***

Flounder With Peanuts

When my parents were on their honeymoon in 1948 in New Orleans, they enjoyed an unusual trout-with-peanuts dish at the famous restaurant Arnaud's. Mom decided to come up with a version of her own at home, and this is her creation. The combination of peanuts and fish might sound a little off-beat, but it seems to win over everybody who tries it.

1 cup chopped salted peanuts
2 tablespoons butter, melted
Salt and pepper
1½ to 2 pounds flounder fillets
Softened butter, to dot on the fish
½ cup Ritz cracker crumbs
Paprika

Preheat the oven to 425 degrees. In a small bowl, stir together the chopped peanuts and the melted butter. Set aside. Salt and pepper the flounder fillets and place them, skin-side down, on a baking sheet. Dot the fillets with the softened butter and sprinkle the Ritz crumbs on top. Place the fish in the oven and bake until the fillets just begin to turn opaque. Sprinkle the top of each fillet with the peanut mixture, then shake a little paprika on top. Continue baking the fish until it is cooked through, watching to make sure the peanuts don't burn. Makes about 4 servings.

Lemon Chicken Legare

½ cup all-purpose flour
1 teaspoon salt
1 teaspoon paprika
8 boneless, skinless chicken breasts
Juice of 3 lemons
3 tablespoons (or more) olive oil
1 cube chicken bouillon
¾ cup boiling water
2 tablespoons brown sugar
¼ cup chopped green onion
Fresh parsley and lemon slices, as garnishes

Everyone I know is looking for something new to do with boneless, skinless chicken breasts, so if you're in the market for an idea, try this recipe from Edie's collection. That lemon zing always says spring to me.

Combine the flour, salt and paprika in a large, resealable plastic bag, mixing well. Place the chicken in a glass bowl and pour the lemon juice on top. Let stand for 10-15 minutes. Remove the chicken; save the lemon juice. Place the chickens breasts, one at a time, in the plastic bag, shaking to coat. Cook the chicken in the olive oil over medium-high heat, turning to brown both sides, until the meat is cooked through. Remove the chicken and place it in a warm oven; save the drippings in the pan. In a 2-cup measure, dissolve the bouillon cube in the boiling water. Stir in the brown sugar and the reserved lemon juice. Pour the mixture into the pan drippings in the skillet and bring it all to a boil, stirring frequently. Reduce the heat and simmer, covered, for 5 minutes, stirring occasionally. Add the onions and simmer, covered, for 10 minutes, stirring occasionally. Serve chicken sauce on top. Garnish with the parsley and lemon slices. Makes 8 servings.

Lowcountry folks will know that the last word in the name of this recipe is pronounced "Luh-GREE" – not "Leh-GAR." It's a fine old Charleston name.

Rosemary Lamb Chops

⅓ cup red wine
⅓ cup lemon juice
⅓ cup canola oil
¼ cup Dijon mustard
½ cup chopped fresh rosemary
4 cloves garlic, minced
Salt and freshly-ground black pepper
12 lamb chops, each about ¾-inch thick

Rosemary winters over very well in our region, so we have a year-round supply. I use it frequently, especially in the early spring when it still gets too chilly at night for my warm-weather favorites, such as basil.

In a mixing bowl, stir together all ingredients except the lamb chops. Place the chops in a large zipper-top plastic bag or a nonreactive dish, and pour the marinade over the top. Refrigerate (covered, if you're using a dish) for 24 hours. When ready to grill, remove the chops from the marinade; discard the marinade. Grill the chops about 5 minutes per side, or until they reach the desired degree of doneness (on an instant-read meat thermometer, 145 degrees is medium-rare, 160 degrees is medium). Makes 6 servings.

Mom's Pound Cake

**3 sticks butter (or 2 sticks butter
and 1 stick margarine), at room temperature
2 cups sugar
5 large eggs, at room temperature
1 teaspoon baking powder
3 cups sifted all-purpose flour
(sift before measuring)
½-¾ cup milk, at room temperature
1 tablespoon vanilla extract
1 or 2 drops almond extract, optional**

Preheat the oven to 350 degrees. Grease and flour a 10-cup tube or bundt pan. In a large mixing bowl, cream the butter until it's soft and fluffy. Add the sugar a little at a time, beating until the mixture is well creamed (scrape down the sides of the bowl as needed throughout the recipe). Add the eggs one at a time, beating before adding the next. Add the baking powder to the flour, then beat about one-third of the flour into the butter-sugar mixture. Beat in about half of the milk. Beat in another third of the flour, then the rest of the milk and the vanilla as well (the almond extract, too, if you're using it). Finish by beating in the remaining flour. Pour the batter into the prepared pan and smooth the top. Bake for 45 minutes. Use a cake tester or toothpick to check for doneness; it should come out clean. If the cake isn't done, continue baking; check every few minutes. It's OK if the cake cracks on top. Remove from the oven and cool on a wire rack for 30 minutes, then remove it from the pan and cool completely. Makes 12-16 servings.

Pound cake originally got its name from its ingredients: a pound of sugar, a pound of butter, a pound of flour and a pound of eggs. That makes a pretty heavy, dense cake, so few modern-day recipes follow that formula.

The recipe I've always sworn by is my mother's. It originated with her grandmother, and Mom has tinkered with it only a little bit. The cake is buttery-rich and has substance. It's lighter than "dense" but it stands up well to anything you might like to serve on the side, such as ice cream or fresh fruit or a dessert sauce (or your favorite combination thereof).

Pound Cake Pointers
– Be sure to have the ingredients at room temperature.
– Bake the cake just below the center of the oven.
– Don't open the oven door for a peak for at least 45 minutes; at that point, check the cake for doneness.

Carolina Thre Coconut C

As if it weren't enough that this cake is delicious – it's also easy to make. In fact, for a family meal or party, it couldn't be more perfect. That's because it needs to be made three days ahead of time – which helps the hostess get one often-time-consuming task out of the way early.

South Carolinians love a good coconut cake, and this one is a favorite in our family. It seems just right for an Easter dinner – and that's when we often enjoy it.

1 (18.5-ounce) box white cake mix (preferably Duncan Hines)
1½ cups sugar
8 ounces sour cream
12 ounces frozen coconut, thawed
1 (8-ounce) tub prepared whipped topping

Prepare the cake mix as the package directs (with egg whites only), using two 9-inch round cake pans. Bake the cake as instructed, then let the layers cool completely. Slice each layer in half horizontally so you have a total of four layers. In a mixing bowl, mix together the sugar, sour cream and coconut. Set aside 1 cup of the mixture. Begin assembling the cake by spreading the remainder of the mixture between the layers. Stir the reserved 1 cup of the coconut mixture into three-quarters of the whipped topping. (Don't use the whole 8 ounces; that makes the frosting too soft to handle. Use 6 ounces only.) Frost the top and sides of the cake with the topping mixture.   Cover the cake and refrigerate it for three days before serving. Store any leftovers in the refrigerator. Makes 16-20 servings.

Some cooks swear by a strand of dental floss for slicing a cake layer in two. Just cut a long length of plain floss and use it to "knife" through the layer for a nice, clean cut.

Mount Pleasant Pluff Mud Brownies

For the cake:

2 sticks butter
2 cups sugar
⅓ cup unsweetened cocoa powder
4 large eggs
1 teaspoon vanilla extract
1½ cups all-purpose flour
1 cup chopped pecans
1 (7-ounce) jar marshmallow creme

For the frosting:

1 stick butter, softened
1 cup unsweetened cocoa powder
6-8 tablespoons milk
1 (16-ounce) box powdered sugar
1 teaspoon vanilla extract
1 cup chopped pecans

*I*f you think mud is mud is mud, you haven't smelled, or squished your toes into, the mud around Charleston. It's called pluff mud here, and it's one of a kind. It's oozy when you sink a foot into it, and it's got a distinctive smell, especially when the weather is warm. Some people wrinkle up their noses at the first sniff, but to me that fragrance means I'm home.

When I was in college in Davidson, N.C., every drive home at the end of the school year in May ended the same way: I saw the marsh and the Cooper River as I turned onto our street, and I took a deep breath of that pluff-muddy air.

I'm just as fond of my sister Edie's Pluff Mud Brownies. They're gooey and oozy and dark and rich, just like the mud for which they're named.

Preheat the oven to 350 degrees. Grease a jellyroll pan (about 15x10x1-inch). To make the cake: in a large bowl, cream together the butter and the sugar, then beat in the cocoa, eggs, vanilla, flour and nuts. Pour into the prepared pan and bake for 20 minutes. Let the cake cool in the pan on a wire rack for about 8-10 minutes, then spread the marshmallow creme over the top (the cake should be warm, but not hot). Continue cooling the cake in pan on the rack.

Carolina Three-Day Coconut Cake

As if it weren't enough that this cake is delicious – it's also easy to make. In fact, for a family meal or party, it couldn't be more perfect. That's because it needs to be made three days ahead of time – which helps the hostess get one often-time-consuming task out of the way early.

South Carolinians love a good coconut cake, and this one is a favorite in our family. It seems just right for an Easter dinner – and that's when we often enjoy it.

1 (18.5-ounce) box white cake mix (preferably Duncan Hines)
1½ cups sugar
8 ounces sour cream
12 ounces frozen coconut, thawed
1 (8-ounce) tub prepared whipped topping

Prepare the cake mix as the package directs (with egg whites only), using two 9-inch round cake pans. Bake the cake as instructed, then let the layers cool completely. Slice each layer in half horizontally so you have a total of four layers. In a mixing bowl, mix together the sugar, sour cream and coconut. Set aside 1 cup of the mixture. Begin assembling the cake by spreading the remainder of the mixture between the layers. Stir the reserved 1 cup of the coconut mixture into three-quarters of the whipped topping. (Don't use the whole 8 ounces; that makes the frosting too soft to handle. Use 6 ounces only.) Frost the top and sides of the cake with the topping mixture. Cover the cake and refrigerate it for three days before serving. Store any leftovers in the refrigerator. Makes 16-20 servings.

Some cooks swear by a strand of dental floss for slicing a cake layer in two. Just cut a long length of plain floss and use it to "knife" through the layer for a nice, clean cut.

Mount Pleasant Pluff Mud Brownies

For the cake:

2 sticks butter
2 cups sugar
⅓ cup unsweetened cocoa powder
4 large eggs
1 teaspoon vanilla extract
1½ cups all-purpose flour
1 cup chopped pecans
1 (7-ounce) jar marshmallow creme

For the frosting:

1 stick butter, softened
1 cup unsweetened cocoa powder
6-8 tablespoons milk
1 (16-ounce) box powdered sugar
1 teaspoon vanilla extract
1 cup chopped pecans

*I*f you think mud is mud is mud, you haven't smelled, or squished your toes into, the mud around Charleston. It's called pluff mud here, and it's one of a kind. It's oozy when you sink a foot into it, and it's got a distinctive smell, especially when the weather is warm. Some people wrinkle up their noses at the first sniff, but to me that fragrance means I'm home.

When I was in college in Davidson, N.C., every drive home at the end of the school year in May ended the same way: I saw the marsh and the Cooper River as I turned onto our street, and I took a deep breath of that pluff-muddy air.

I'm just as fond of my sister Edie's Pluff Mud Brownies. They're gooey and oozy and dark and rich, just like the mud for which they're named.

Preheat the oven to 350 degrees. Grease a jellyroll pan (about 15x10x1-inch). To make the cake: in a large bowl, cream together the butter and the sugar, then beat in the cocoa, eggs, vanilla, flour and nuts. Pour into the prepared pan and bake for 20 minutes. Let the cake cool in the pan on a wire rack for about 8-10 minutes, then spread the marshmallow creme over the top (the cake should be warm, but not hot). Continue cooling the cake in pan on the rack.

To make the frosting: in a mixing bowl, using an electric mixer, blend the butter, cocoa, milk, powdered sugar and vanilla. (Start with 6 tablespoons of the milk, adding the extra a little bit at a time until the frosting is of a good, spreadable consistency). Stir in the nuts. Spread the frosting over the marshmallow layer on the cake. Cut into squares (about 3x3 inches) to serve on plates, or cut into smaller squares for eating out of hand. Makes 16-20 servings.

Hummingbird Cake

When the azaleas, dogwood and wisteria wash churchyards in a palette of spring pastels, a number of local church congregations serve light "tearoom" lunches at their parish halls as fund-raisers for their ministries. The hands-down highlight of any tearoom is dessert. The ladies of the church spend hours each day baking their best made-from-scratch cakes, pies and more.

For the cake:

3 cups all-purpose flour
2 cups sugar
1 teaspoon baking soda
1 teaspoon salt
1 teaspoon ground cinnamon
1 cup vegetable oil
3 large eggs
1½ teaspoons vanilla extract
1 (8-ounce) can crushed pineapple, undrained
2 cups mashed, over-ripe bananas
1 cup chopped pecans, optional

For the frosting:

12 ounces cream cheese, softened
1½ sticks butter, softened
1½ teaspoons vanilla extract
1½ (16-ounce) boxes powdered sugar
½ cup chopped pecans (or some pretty pecan halves), as a garnish

Preheat the oven to 350 degrees. Grease and flour three 9-inch round cake pans, or one jelly-roll pan (11x15x2 inches). To make the cake: sift the first five ingredients together into a large bowl. Add the oil, eggs, vanilla, pineapple, bananas and pecans; stir to combine. Spoon the batter into the pans. Bake 25-30 minutes, or until a toothpick inserted in the center comes out clean. Cool in the pans on a rack. If using round pans, remove the layers after 10 minutes; let them finish cooling on rack.

For the frosting: beat the cream cheese, butter and vanilla until creamy, then gradually beat in the powdered sugar. Frost the cake between the layers, on the sides and top. Sprinkle the chopped nuts on top, or arrange the halves decoratively. Makes 12-14 servings.

Hummingbird Cake is a favorite year after year. The recipe originally appeared in Southern Living in 1978 as a three-layer cake, and it's a show-stopper. But we sometimes make this in a jelly-roll pan for easy transporting to any get-together. We've tinkered with the recipe a bit in other ways — making a little more frosting, and sprinkling the nuts on top rather than stirring them into the frosting.

Lemon Blitz Torte

For the cake:

½ cup butter
¾ cup powdered sugar
4 large egg yolks, slightly beaten
1 teaspoon vanilla extract
1 cup all-purpose flour
¼ teaspoon salt
1 teaspoon baking powder
¼ cup milk

For the meringue:

4 large egg whites
¼ teaspoon cream of tartar

The layer of zesty lemon filling in this pretty cake makes it distinctive. The recipe came down to this generation from my paternal grandmother, St. Clair Mitchell.

¾ cup granulated sugar
⅓ cup sliced blanched almonds or pecans

For the filling:

1 cup granulated sugar
3 tablespoons cornstarch
½ teaspoon salt
2 large egg yolks, slightly beaten
Juice of 2 lemons, plus grated rind of one lemon
1 cup water
2 tablespoons butter

Preheat the oven to 350 degrees. Thoroughly grease two 9-inch cake pans. To make the cake: cream the butter and powdered sugar. Add the yolks and vanilla. Measure the flour into a sifter; add salt and baking powder, then sift. Add the flour to the butter mixture alternately with the milk, beginning and ending with the flour. Spread in the prepared pans. Beat the egg whites with the cream of tartar until soft peaks form. Slowly add the granulated sugar, beating until stiff peaks form. Lightly spread this meringue over the cake batter and sprinkle with nuts. Bake 25-30 minutes, or until the meringue is golden. Cool in the pans on racks for 10 minutes, then turn out on racks, meringue side up, and cool thoroughly.

To make the filling, mix the sugar, cornstarch and salt in a saucepan. Add the egg yolks, lemon juice. rind and water. Cook over low heat, stirring constantly, until thickened, then stir in the butter. Let cool, then spread half on top of the meringue on one cake layer. Place the other layer carefully on top, then spread the remaining filling over the meringue. Makes 12-14 servings.

Buttermilk Pie

**1 stick butter, softened
2 cups sugar
3 tablespoons all-purpose flour
3 large eggs, beaten
1 cup buttermilk
1 tablespoon vanilla or lemon extract
Dash of nutmeg (optional; can also sprinkle on
top just before baking if desired)
2 unbaked 9-inch pastry pie shells**

This makes a light, cooling dessert to serve on a warm day. My mother was given the recipe years ago by friends in North Carolina.

Preheat the oven to 350 degrees. Using an electric mixer, cream the butter and sugar until light and fluffy. Beat in the flour, then the eggs, until combined. Beat in the buttermilk, extract and nutmeg (if using). Divide the mixture between the two pie shells; sprinkle nutmeg on top if desired. Bake for 45-50 minutes. Makes 2 pies, about 6-8 servings per pie.

Grasshopper Pie

The coolness of mint always makes me think about spring, and this refreshing, minty pie not only tastes like spring, it looks like spring, too, with its pretty light-mint color. It gets its name from the cocktail with similar ingredients.

This would make a nice addition to an Easter dessert buffet.

1 (6-ounce) package semisweet chocolate morsels
1 tablespoon shortening
1½ cups finely-chopped pecans
About 35 large marshmallows
⅓ cup milk
¼ teaspoon salt
3 tablespoons crème de menthe
3 tablespoons white crème de cacao
1½ cups heavy cream, whipped
Additional whipped cream, plus chocolate shavings and fresh mint leaves, as a garnish (optional)

Line a 9-inch pie plate with aluminum foil (the foil should come up and over the edges of the pan). In the top of a double boiler set over simmering water, place the chocolate morsels and the shortening. Stir until the morsels melt. Stir in the nuts. Pour the mixture evenly over the bottom and brush it up the sides of the foil-lined plate. Chill for 1 hour. Remove the pie plate from the refrigerator and, using the aluminum foil that hangs over the edges, gently lift the chocolate shell out of the pan. Peel off the foil carefully, then put the chocolate shell on a serving plate. Cover and refrigerate again. In the (clean) double boiler, set over simmering water, combine the marshmallows, milk and salt. Stir until the marshmallows melt. Remove the pan from the heat and stir in the crème de menthe and crème de cacao. Chill the mixture for about 1 hour, until slightly thickened, then fold in the whipped cream. Pour the filling into the chilled chocolate shell, then refrigerate for about 1 hour, or until firm. Garnish with whipped cream, chocolate shavings or fresh mint leaves, if desired. Makes about 8 servings.

Lemon Thyme Shortbread

2 sticks butter, softened
2 tablespoons finely-chopped lemon thyme leaves
¼ cup powdered sugar
¼ cup granulated sugar
2½ cups all-purpose flour
1 to 2 teaspoons orange flower water or rose water

Preheat the oven to 325 degrees. Cream the butter and the lemon thyme together for 30 seconds. Add the sugars and cream until light. Add half the flour and mix on medium speed until well blended. Add the remaining flour and mix until the dough is crumbly, but begins to hold together. Add the orange flower water and mix for another 10 seconds. Take a tablespoon of dough and squeeze it in your palm to make it hold together well, then roll it into a ball. Put the ball on an ungreased cookie sheet and flatten with a cookie press or the bottom of a glass (if using a glass, press a design onto the cookie with a fork or a miniature cookie cutter or canape cutter – but don't cut all the way through or the cookie will break when baked). Bake the cookies for 20-25 minutes. Cool 10 minutes before moving to a wire rack to cool completely.

The springtime taste of the herb lemon thyme adds a wonderful burst of flavor to these classic shortbread cookies. Caroline Madsen, who owns Pete's Herbs with her husband, Pete, shared the recipe for these cookies several years ago at a local class on using herbs in desserts. I've made these many times, and they never fail to please.

Be sure to chop the lemon thyme leaves very fine for these buttery cookies.

Keep It Simple Strawberry Dip

When fresh strawberries signal the arrival of spring, we stock up on them by the bucket-ful. This easy dipping sauce is just right with the fat, sweet berries. It enhances them but doesn't overwhelm them.

The recipe here is just a starting point; adjust the ratio of sour cream and brown sugar to your taste.

1 cup sour cream
¼ cup (packed) light brown sugar
1 or 2 drops vanilla extract

Stir all ingredients together in a bowl. Refrigerate until the sauce is well chilled. Serve with whole fresh strawberries for dipping, or spoon a dollop of the sauce on top of a bowl of sliced berries. Makes 1 cup.

Lemon Lovies

For the crust:

1 stick butter, at room temperature
1 cup all-purpose flour
¼ cup powdered sugar

For the lemon layer:

1 cup granulated sugar
2 tablespoons all-purpose flour
½ teaspoon baking powder
2 large eggs
Juice and finely-grated rind (zest) of 1 lemon
Extra powdered sugar, for dusting

Preheat oven to 350 degrees. Lightly grease an 8-inch square baking pan. To make the crust: in a bowl, mix together the softened butter, the flour and the powdered sugar. Pat into the bottom of the pan. Bake for 12-15 minutes, just until light golden brown. Remove the pan from the oven and place it on a wire rack.

To make the lemon layer: combine the sugar, flour, baking powder, eggs, lemon juice and rind. Pour the mixture on top of the warm baked crust. Return the pan to the oven and bake for 20 minutes more. Remove from oven and cool completely on a wire rack before cutting into squares. Add a light dusting of powdered sugar, if desired, before serving. Makes 16 squares, 2x2 inches each.

These bar cookies with a shortbread-like crust provide a bright, lemon-tart finish to a simple lunch or picnic. To fancy them up for a company's-coming occasion, cut the bars small and place them in pretty paper muffin-cup liners, with a light dusting with powdered sugar on top.

Served on a silver tray, they look quite pretty, like a ray of spring sunshine. My sister was given this recipe years ago by a Charleston friend, Lisa Menefee.

To keep a dusting of powdered sugar light and lump-free, place the sugar in a hand-held, fine-mesh sieve. Hold the sieve over the bars and tap ever so lightly on the rim of the sieve. This ensures that the powdered sugar does, indeed, look like a dusting, rather than a dumping.

Vanilla Ice Cream

*T*opped with warm chocolate sauce, this dessert is like the spring weather in South Carolina — a little bit chilly starting out, with a wonderful warm-up topping things off.

4 large eggs
1 cup sugar
5 cups milk
2 tablespoons cornstarch
⅓ cup very cold water
1 tablespoon vanilla extract
1 pint whipping cream

Combine the eggs and the sugar in a large bowl. Beat well with a whisk, then set aside. In the top of a double boiler over simmering water, heat the milk until it's very hot (but don't let it boil). Pour the hot milk slowly, a little at a time, into the egg mixture, whisking as you go. Pour the mixture back into the double boiler and cook it slowly, stirring constantly, until it thickens slightly, enough to lightly coat the back of a spoon. In a small bowl, stir together the cornstarch and cold water, then add it to the custard mixture in the double-boiler. Stir, and when the custard becomes thicker, take it off the heat immediately and strain it into a bowl. Stir in the vanilla. Chill the custard thoroughly. When you're ready to make the ice cream, remove the custard from the refrigerator and stir in the chilled whipping cream. Churn the ice cream according to the instructions for your ice cream maker. Serve with Warm Chocolate Sauce. Makes about 3 quarts.

Warm Chocolate Sauce

**4 ounces good-quality semisweet chocolate,
coarsely chopped
½ cup milk
½ cup sugar
½ cup light corn syrup
2 tablespoons butter, softened
½ teaspoon vanilla extract**

In a saucepan set over low heat, combine the chocolate and the milk, stirring until the chocolate melts. Add the sugar, corn syrup and butter one at a time, in the order given, stirring after each addition until the mixture is smooth. Continue to cook over low heat for 5 minutes. Remove the pan from the heat and stir in the vanilla. Serve warm over ice cream (or cake, such as pound cake). Makes about 1⅓ cups.

Summer

Summer

S outh Carolina summers served as the perfect stove top where afternoon storms brewed and boiled and rose like thunderous battalions that drove little boys from the playing fields to the shelter of porches, where we often found our mothers' love in the form of food.

Oftentimes, as we watched distant lightning dance along the horizon, our fears were calmed by the soothing taste of popsicles, red and grape and orange, broken in half and licked down to the wooden stick as the flavors dripped like the oncoming rain down our chins and fingers.

As children of the sun, our hair was bleached and our young bodies tanned by the long days that stretched from the last day of school to the first days of football. In between was a lazy monotony of dew-dappled mornings that were quickly sautéed by the sun. By noon the heat was high and a gaggle of sandlot baseball boys would come flying through someone's screen porch and collect around the kitchen table, where gallons of sweet iced tea would disappear faster than peanut butter sandwiches could be made.

If heat and humidity forged our Southern souls, our hearts were certainly tenderized by the bounty of our land.

Although our air was conditioned some time later, those whirring machines never had the capacity to cool down a little boy's body like wedges of watermelon chilled in a washtub of ice. To sink your sunburned face into a crescent-shaped slice was a polar experience in the midst of a hothouse. To feel the juices running down your neck and chest was a true joy of childhood.

Such was a time and place where neighbors left fresh-picked vegetables on your back stoop. It was an unpretentious act of kindness.

Occasionally, on Friday evenings, I would go with my father into the country where men stood around gurgling pots of oil, smoking cigarettes and sipping whiskey from small bottles. There in the cauldron roiled breaded panfish like bream and crappie and catfish that curled when they were cooked.

One by one they were plucked out and plopped on paper plates with slaw and hushpuppies and we would sit on logs and overturned gas cans and slide the freshwater meat off the spiny frames and fling the boney carcasses into the darkness beyond the campfire.

Sometimes, on Sundays after church, under a shade tree, we would take turns churning homemade ice cream in a silver cylinder that magically frosted up on the outside as the contents thickened and our little arms tired to the task.

And there, in the haze of those long-lost afternoons, we ate peach ice cream until our entire bodies were sticky and mothers had to hose us down in the back yard – just before a summer storm came up and washed our tiny footprints away.

Crock-Pot Boiled Peanuts

2 pounds fresh green peanuts, in the shell
½ cup kosher salt (or ⅓ cup regular salt)

Rinse the peanuts well and place them in a Crock-Pot (3 quarts or larger). Sprinkle the salt over the peanuts, then cover them with water. Place the lid on the Crock-Pot and set the temperature to high. Cook for 7 hours, then take a few peanuts out of their shells, taste, and adjust the salt if needed. Cook for 8-10 hours total (the peanuts shouldn't get mushy). They're best if served warm, but leftovers (if there are any) can be refrigerated and will keep for several days.

The hardest thing about this recipe is figuring out how many people it will serve. As a tailgating or pre-picnic snack, I'd say it serves anywhere from 4 to 8 people. My husband, who loves boiled peanuts, says this recipe will serve one!

If you live in the South, you probably know what boiled peanuts are. If you don't live in the South, you might never have heard of them – and you might not like how they sound. But let me encourage you to keep an open mind and try this recipe. I predict you'll end up addicted! Boiled peanuts are simply fresh green peanuts, cooked long and slow in water and salt (and occasionally some other seasoning). When the peanuts are nice and tender, just break open the shell and pop the peanuts in your mouth. Southerners scarf them down by the bowlful at picnics, cookouts, fairs, tailgate parties or just sitting around the house watching TV.

Crock-Pots are ideal for making boiled peanuts – no fuss, no muss. The salt amounts below are easy to crank up – after the peanuts cook for about 7 hours, just taste a few and add more salt if you like. In my experience, it takes about 15-20 minutes for the added salt to "sink in."

Cooper River Crab Dip

A late summer afternoon often finds much of our family gathered on Aunt Jean Mitchell's porch. Her rambling Mount Pleasant house is right on the waterfront, with a spectacular view out into Charleston Harbor. We watch the boats go by – everything from one-seater sailboats to the monstrous container ships heading for the Port of Charleston. My favorite boats to watch are the shrimp trawlers heading back into Shem Creek, the traditional home of the shrimp industry in the Lowcountry. The crews on the boats are often sorting through their catch and tossing the small "trash fish" over the side – which lures dozens upon dozens of gulls to follow in their wake, diving for an easy dinner. Now that's the catch of the day!

2 (8-ounce) packages cream cheese, softened
⅓ cup mayonnaise
1 tablespoon powdered sugar
1 tablespoon dry white wine, such as Chablis
½ teaspoon onion juice
½ teaspoon prepared mustard
¾ teaspoon garlic salt
¼ teaspoon salt
1 cup fresh crabmeat
Chopped fresh parsley

In a mixing bowl, stir together all ingredients except for the crabmeat and parsley; mix well. Gently stir in the crabmeat. Spoon the mixture into a lightly greased, 1-quart baking dish. Bake at 375 degrees for 15 minutes. Remove from the oven, sprinkle with parsley and serve warm with assorted crackers. Makes about 2¾ cups.

For those of us watching from the porch, the catch of the day is always Aunt Jean's crab dip — we've been known to make supper out of it some nights.

While most of the country pronounces "Cooper" as "KOO-per" Charlestonians say "KUH-pah" instead. If we can do that to a simple word like "Cooper," just imagine what we do to the good old Lowcountry family name Vanderhorst. (It's VAN-dross if you couldn't guess.)

Shrimp Paste

1 pound shrimp, cooked and peeled
6-8 tablespoons mayonnaise
Salt and white pepper, to taste
Dash of red pepper or Tabasco sauce

*M*y family has tried many versions of shrimp paste, and we keep coming back to this one for its simplicity, and for the way it lets the wonderful taste of fresh shrimp shine through.

Pulse the shrimp several times in a food processor. They should be in small pieces, but don't pulverize them; the shrimp paste should have some texture. Stir together the shrimp and the remaining ingredients. Cover and chill completely before serving with crackers. Makes about 2 cups.

Shrimp paste looks nice when it's shaped into a half-ball on a platter, with crackers arranged around the edge. Sprinkle a bit of paprika on top of the paste if you wish; it adds a nice color.

Dockside Crab Dip

*A*nother recipe
clipped from the newspaper
ages ago, this cool, rich
dip can easily be doubled
for a larger crowd.

1 (8-ounce) package cream cheese, softened
½ cup mayonnaise
¼ cup finely-grated cheddar cheese
1 small garlic clove, pressed
1 teaspoon Worcestershire sauce
Salt and freshly-ground black pepper, to taste
1 cup fresh crabmeat, shredded

In a mixing bowl, beat together the cream cheese and
mayonnaise with an electric mixer. Stir in the remaining ingredients. Chill until ready to serve. Serve with
assorted crackers. Makes approximately 1 cup.

Aunt Jean's Hot Pepper Jelly

2 cups water
6-10 teaspoons Tabasco sauce (red)
⅔ cup fresh lemon juice
6 cups sugar
1 (6-ounce) bottle pectin
Red or green food coloring

In a large saucepan, mix the water, Tabasco, lemon juice and sugar. Bring to a boil, stirring constantly. Add the pectin and food coloring (to desired tint) and bring to a rolling boil. Boil 2 minutes, then remove from the heat and skim any foam off the top. Pour in sterilized jars, then seal. Serve with cream cheese on crackers. Makes about 6 half-pint jars.

There's something about hot weather that makes me a fan of hot (as in spicy) food, which I usually approach with much caution. What I like best about Aunt Jean's Hot Pepper Jelly is the way the heat of the jelly and the cool of the accompanying cream cheese play off each other.

This appetizer always reminds me of late-summer afternoons on the porch, looking over the waterfront. If you make a red batch and a green batch, the two look pretty on a party tray.

Tasty Zucchini Bread

This recipe has been in the family collection for years. I think it came from the newspaper, but its source beyond that is a mystery to me.

3 cups all-purpose flour
1 teaspoon salt
1 teaspoon baking soda
1 tablespoon baking powder
1 tablespoon ground cinnamon
3 large eggs
2 cups firmly-packed light brown sugar
2 cups shredded zucchini (peel on)
¾ cup vegetable oil
2 teaspoons vanilla extract

Preheat the oven to 350 degrees. Grease and flour one 9x5-inch loaf pan, or two 8x4-inch loaf pans. In a mixing bowl, whisk together the flour, salt, baking soda, baking powder and cinnamon. In another bowl, using an electric mixer, beat the eggs and sugar together until they're combined. Stir in the shredded zucchini, oil and vanilla. Add the flour mixture to the egg mixture, stirring just until the ingredients are well-combined. Spread the batter in the prepared pan(s). Bake 65-70 minutes for 1 loaf (or 40-45 minutes for 2 loaves), until a toothpick inserted in the center comes out clean. Cool the bread in the pan(s) on a wire rack for 10 minutes, then remove it from the pan and finish cooling on the rack. Makes 1 large or 2 smaller loaves. If you're using glass baking pans, reduce the baking temperature to 325 degrees.

John's Island Tomato Ketchup

**7 pounds ripe but firm tomatoes, peeled, seeded
and finely chopped
1 teaspoon salt
¾ cup sugar
3 whole cloves
3 dried bay leaves (or 5 fresh bay leaves)
¾ teaspoon ground coriander
1 stick cinnamon
1 tablespoon dry mustard
4 cloves garlic, very finely minced
½ teaspoon freshly-ground black pepper
1¼ cups cider vinegar**

Place all the ingredients in a heavy-bottomed stainless steel pot and stir to combine. Bring to a steady boil, stirring occasionally, then reduce the heat to a simmer. Cook for 1 hour, stirring occasionally to keep ketchup from scorching, until the ketchup thickens. Remove the cloves, bay leaves and the cinnamon stick. Cool, then refrigerate in a tightly-closed jar or container. (If you like a very smooth ketchup, you can puree it before refrigerating.) The ketchup keeps very well, refrigerated, for 10 months. Makes about 3-4 cups.

*I*t's hard for me to resist trying to make a homemade version of something we usually buy in stores. (Well, it's a little easier than it used to be, thanks to a disastrous attempt to try to make jellybeans at home – who knew I'd need a centrifuge?) When I saw a ketchup recipe in **The Fog City Diner Cookbook** (Ten Speed Press, 1993), I had to give it a shot. The recipe below is what evolved from that after much tinkering.

I cut back drastically on the sugar – from 2 cups down to 3/4 cup – and slightly on the vinegar, while increasing the garlic and most of the spices. With hamburgers and hot dogs fresh off the grill, this is terrific.

When seeding the tomatoes, cut out any white, fibrous-looking parts; they detract from the beautiful color of the finished product. Same with the garlic – if it's not very finely chopped, you'll end up with little white flecks in the ketchup.
   Sometimes tomatoes can be watery. Drain off any accumulated juices from the chopped tomatoes before adding them to the pot. The tomatoes will give up more liquid as they cook; you can drain that off if you want.

Grape Tomato and Butter Bean Salad

Holly Herrick, the restaurant reviewer for **The Post and Courier,** came up with this delicious salad when she was working on a summer farmers' market story for our food section, and it's one of my favorite recipes in this book.

The butter beans and grape tomatoes are terrific partners, and the tangy blue cheese and toasted pecans add their own distinctive touches. The balsamic vinegar brings everything together smoothly.

This is a great side dish for anything off the grill — or you can dress it up for a nice brunch or lunch by hollowing out a fat fresh tomato and serving the salad inside it.

Grape tomatoes have been red-hot at our farmers' markets for the past few years. They're red like tomatoes, but they're shaped like green grapes — and are just about as sweet!

3 cups butter beans, rinsed and drained
1 tablespoon salt
2½ cups grape tomatoes, halved
Half a red onion, finely chopped
¼ cup olive oil
2 tablespoons balsamic vinegar
10 leaves fresh basil, chopped
Salt and freshly-ground black pepper, to taste
¼ cup crumbled blue cheese (optional garnish)
½ cup pecan halves (optional garnish)
2 tablespoons olive oil (optional garnish)

Place the butter beans in a large pot; cover with water and add 1 tablespoon salt. Bring to a boil, then reduce to a simmer and cook until tender, about 30 minutes. Drain, rinse and set aside to cool. In a large salad bowl, stir together the butter beans and all the remaining ingredients except the optional garnishes. Taste and check for seasonings. Cover and let the flavors blend at room temperature for 1 hour. Meanwhile, if using the pecan halves, place them in a small sauté pan with the 2 tablespoons olive oil, plus salt and pepper to taste, if desired. Place the pan over medium-high heat; toss or stir the pecans constantly to prevent burning. When the pecans are toasted, fragrant and golden in color, remove them from the heat and place them on paper towels to cool. To serve, spoon the salad onto plates or into bowls, then sprinkle the warm pecans and crumbled blue cheese over the top. Makes 6-8 servings.

Shem Creek Pasta Salad

**1 (12-ounce) package roasted garlic and
red pepper fettuccine
4 to 8 ounces feta cheese, crumbled
Half of a sweet onion, finely chopped
3 cups quartered cherry tomatoes (or halved
grape tomatoes)
10 fresh basil leaves, sliced into thin strips**

For the balsamic vinaigrette:

**¼ cup balsamic vinegar
1 heaping teaspoon Dijon mustard
2 cloves garlic, minced
¾ cup olive oil**

Tomatoes and basil are a match made in heaven, and no home garden plot in the Lowcountry is complete without its share of both. Flavored pasta – in this case, roasted garlic and red pepper – is a convenient way to add even more flavor to the mix. Edie contributed this recipe to Tested By Time, the cookbook published by the Parents Association at Porter-Gaud School.

Break the pasta into bite-size pieces and cook according to package directions, just until tender. Drain, rinse in cold water, then drain again. In a bowl, stir together the pasta, cheese, onion, tomatoes and basil. To make the vinaigrette: combine the vinegar, mustard and garlic in a blender container. While blending at high speed, add the olive oil in a fine stream, blending constantly until mixture is smooth. To serve, add as much of the vinaigrette as desired to the salad; stir gently. Serve salad warm. Makes 6 servings.

Fresh Tuna Salad

*I*f you've never tasted tuna salad made with fresh-caught tuna, you're in for a treat. Pile this on a bed of lettuce and some sliced, home-grown tomatoes, or turn it into a heckuva good tuna salad sandwich.

1 pound fresh tuna medallions
Salt, to taste
1 tablespoon whole black peppercorns
One-quarter of a small onion
5 ribs celery, divided
⅓ cup mayonnaise
Seasoned pepper, to taste
Juice of one-half lemon
¼ teaspoon English mustard paste
¼ teaspoon Worcestershire sauce

Place the tuna medallions in a deep skillet and cover with water. Add the salt, peppercorns and onion. Cut two ribs of the celery into several chunks and add them to the pan. Simmer until the tuna is cooked through. Remove from the heat and let the tuna cool, then use a fork to break it into bite-size pieces. Refrigerate. In a small bowl, mix together the mayonnaise, seasoned pepper, lemon juice, mustard paste, Worcestershire and salt. Combine with the tuna. Cut the remaining 3 ribs of celery into small slices, then stir them into the salad. Chill thoroughly before serving. Makes 3-4 servings.

Andy's Jalapeño Corn Bread

2 tablespoons bacon fat (or butter)
1 (8.5-ounce) can cream-style corn
2 cups corn meal (white or yellow)
3 large eggs
1 teaspoon salt
½ teaspoon baking soda
¾ cup milk
⅓ cup corn oil
1 cup grated sharp cheddar cheese
¼ cup chopped jalapeño peppers, veins and seeds removed
2 cups fresh corn kernels

Preheat the oven to 400 degrees. Place the bacon fat or butter in a 9-inch cast iron skillet (or 9-inch baking dish), and put the skillet in the oven. Meanwhile, in a mixing bowl, combine the cream-style corn, cornmeal, eggs, salt, baking soda, milk, oil, ½ cup of the cheese, the jalapeños and the corn kernels. When the butter or fat in the skillet is quite hot—near smoking — immediately pour in the batter; it will sizzle, forming a crispy crust. Sprinkle the remaining cheese on top and bake for 40 minutes, until the cornbread is firm and golden brown. Makes 8-10 servings.

The Post and Courier is lucky to have its own wine and spirits columnist. Andy Felt's full-time job is serving as the director of the Joseph P. Riley Institute for Urban Affairs at the College of Charleston. But he's also written about wine and taught classes on the subject for many years, and he shares his insight twice a month in a column for our food section. It was Andy's approachable and down-to-earth style of writing and talking about wine that sparked my interest in the subject.

Andy's quite a talented cook, and it's just as much fun to talk with him about food as it is to talk about wine. He passed along this recipe, and I made one little addition – some fresh sweet-corn kernels.

"This makes a really good base for a stuffing," Andy tells me. "I've used it for oyster stuffing, and for one made with andouille sausage. Even people who don't like jalapeños seem to like it. Baking will tone down the heat of the pepper quite a bit, but this will still be spicy, so you can use less and gradually work up to your preference."

Stuffed Herbed Tomatoes

*A*unt Jean gave me this recipe. With fresh herbs and the fattest local tomatoes from the market, it's a winner all the way around.

6 medium-size tomatoes
Salt, to taste
¼ cup plus 2 tablespoons fine dry bread crumbs
1 small clove garlic, minced
3 tablespoons chopped onion
1½ teaspoons chopped fresh parsley
¾ teaspoon celery seed
2 tablespoons chopped fresh basil leaves
Freshly-ground black pepper, to taste
Chopped fresh parsley, to garnish

Preheat the oven to 350 degrees. Slice off the tops of the tomatoes, then scoop out the pulp, leaving the shells hollowed out. Chop the pulp and place it in a small bowl; set it aside. Sprinkle salt inside the tomatoes and turn them upside-down to drain. Combine the tomato pulp with the remainder of the ingredients (except the extra parsley for garnish); stir to mix. Fill the tomato shells with the bread crumb mixture and sprinkle the extra chopped fresh parsley on top. Place the tomatoes on a baking sheet and bake for 10-15 minutes. Makes 6 servings.

Green Beans, Sweet Onions, New Potatoes and Diced Tomatoes

1 tablespoon salt
2 bay leaves
½ pound small new potatoes, washed and sliced but not peeled
1 tablespoon chicken stock, homemade or canned low-sodium
1 tablespoon dry white wine
¾ cup olive oil
½ cup red wine vinegar
1 tablespoon Dijon mustard
¾ teaspoon salt, or to taste
¼ teaspoon freshly-ground black pepper
½ pound small green beans, tails and tips off
1 sweet onion, thinly sliced
1 large vine-ripened tomato, seeded and diced
¾ cup chopped fresh parsley

Bring a saucepan of water to a boil over medium-high heat. Add the salt and bay leaves. Add the potatoes, reduce the heat to medium and simmer until just tender, about 8-10 minutes. Drain and immediately toss the hot potatoes gently with the chicken stock and wine. Whisk together the oil, vinegar, Dijon mustard, salt and pepper. Add ¼ cup of the mixture to the potatoes and toss gently. Bring a saucepan of water to a boil over medium-high heat. Add the green beans, reduce the heat to medium and simmer the green

*E*ven the name of this salad says summer in Charleston. The recipe comes from Marion Sullivan, a cookbook consultant who writes a monthly column on new cookbooks for **The Post and Courier.** She says, "This salad was inspired by a classic Salade Niçoise, which features tuna and also includes Niçoise olives and sliced or chopped hard-boiled eggs. A composed salad, Salade Niçoise is presented with the ingredients arranged in rows. If I'm having company, I like to arrange this one, too, with the sliced new potatoes in a circle around the outside, followed by a circle of onions, and the green beans in the center. Sprinkle the diced tomatoes and parsley over the top."

beans until just tender, about 3-4 minutes, depending on the size of the green beans. Drain and rinse under cold water to stop further cooking. When cool, drain well and place on paper towels to dry. When ready to serve, toss the green beans, onion and tomatoes with the dressing. Gently add the potatoes and parsley. Place in a serving bowl. (Or, make a composed salad by arranging the vegetables on a platter as suggested above.) Serve immediately. Makes 6 servings.

Sweet Onion Casserole

The state of Georgia claims the one-and-only Vidalia onion, but in South Carolina we treat them like our own — we love them! Aunt Jean, who has a great collection of microwave recipes, shared this recipe.

2 pounds sweet onions, such as Vidalias, chopped
¼ cup dry white wine
3 tablespoons butter
3 tablespoons all-purpose flour
1 teaspoon chopped fresh chives
½ teaspoon dry mustard
½ teaspoon salt
1 cup milk
½ cup sour cream
1 cup shredded cheddar cheese

Combine the onions, wine and butter in a 2-quart, microwave-safe dish. Cover and cook on high in the microwave for 10-12 minutes, stirring once halfway through. Stir in the flour, chives, mustard and salt; microwave on high for 30 seconds. Slowly stir in the milk and the sour cream; microwave on high for 4-6 minutes, until thickened. Sprinkle the cheddar on top and microwave on medium for 4-6 minutes more, until the cheese melts. Makes about 6 servings.

Super Tomatoes

4 large, fully-ripe tomatoes
Salt and freshly-ground black pepper, to taste
6 large leaves fresh basil, chopped
1 teaspoon freshly-squeezed lime juice
½ teaspoon sugar
1 clove garlic, minced
1 tablespoon olive oil
Fresh parsley and basil leaves, for garnish

Peel the tomatoes, if desired, and slice into ½-inch-thick slices. Arrange them on a serving platter and season them lightly with salt and pepper. Scatter the chopped basil over the tomatoes, then sprinkle the lime juice on top. Mix the sugar, garlic and olive oil, then sprinkle the mixture over the tomatoes. Cover the platter and let the tomatoes stand at least 15 minutes before serving. Garnish with fresh parsley and basil leaves. Makes 6 servings.

We usually have a casual supper on Aunt Jean's porch a couple of times a summer. Ken and my brother-in-law, Andy Blair, take charge of the grill for steaks, the kids run around and play, Dad takes care of the drinks and the ladies each contribute a dish. Super Tomatoes are a staple of those evenings.

These tomatoes are so simple and so fresh, and so perfect with the basil, that hardly anything else is needed for an easy supper.

"These look lovely on a large, flat dish," Mom says. "Garnish them with fresh parsley and basil leaves if you have an herb garden."

Spicy Corn on the Cob

A touch of
Tabasco gives fresh sweet corn an eye-opening new flavor. This is a very easy change of pace from corn on the cob with regular ol' butter – not that there's a thing wrong with that, of course!

This is one of Aunt Jean's microwave recipes, clipped from a magazine a while back.

¼ cup butter
1 teaspoon seasoned salt
⅛ teaspoon freshly-ground black pepper
¼ teaspoon Tabasco
4 ears fresh corn, husks and silks removed

Place the butter in a 1-cup glass measure. Microwave on high for 45-55 seconds, or until melted. Stir in the seasoned salt, pepper and Tabasco. Brush the corn generously with the spicy melted butter, then wrap each ear in heavy-duty plastic wrap. Place the corn in a microwave-safe baking dish and microwave on high for 8-9 minutes, giving the dish a quarter-turn after 4 minutes of cooking time. Unwrap carefully and serve. Makes 4 servings.

Curried Summer Tomato Soup

2 teaspoons olive oil
½ cup chopped sweet onion, such as Vidalia
1 clove garlic, minced
¾ teaspoon curry powder
1½ pounds ripe tomatoes, peeled, halved, cored and seeded
1½ cups chicken broth
½ teaspoon fines herbes, crushed
Salt and freshly-ground black pepper, to taste

Curry powder gives an unusual flavor to this fresh tomato soup. You can serve it warm or chilled. It's particularly refreshing served chilled on a hot day, with a bit of sour cream or plain yogurt dolloped in the center. You can add a sprinkle of fresh thyme leaves, too, if you wish.

In a saucepan heat the oil until hot. Add the onion and garlic and cook until the onions are tender but not browned. Add the curry powder and cook, stirring, for 1 minute. Add the remainder of the ingredients, then bring the mixture to a boil. Reduce the heat, cover and simmer for 10 minutes. Remove from heat. Let the soup cool to lukewarm, then process it in two batches in a food processor or blender until the mixture is smooth. To serve the soup warm, return it to a saucepan and heat through over low heat, or refrigerate, covered, and serve when thoroughly chilled. Makes 6 side-dish servings.

Pearl's Peas

This is an unusual salad — green peas, green beans and onions served chilled with a sweet/sour dressing. We particularly like it with ham.

Since this is a cold side dish, you might want to serve it in a separate bowl or plate, rather than with the hot food on your dinner plate.

1 (14½ ounce) can tiny sweet green peas, drained
1 (14½ ounce) can French-cut green beans, drained
1 (6-ounce) can sliced mushrooms, drained
1 (2-ounce) jar chopped pimiento
1 large sweet onion, sliced very thin and separated into half-rings
1 cup white vinegar
½ cup sugar (or more, to taste)
½ cup vegetable oil

Combine the peas, beans, mushrooms, pimientoes and onions in a large bowl. In a smaller bowl, stir together the vinegar, sugar and oil, stirring until the sugar dissolves. Pour the vinegar mixture over the vegetables and stir gently to coat. Cover and refrigerate for at least 8 hours before serving. Serve with a slotted spoon (to drain off some of the liquid). Makes 6 servings.

This salad will keep well in the refrigerator, covered, for up to one week.

Peach Chutney

4 cups coarsely-chopped, ripe peaches, with juices
⅔ cup apple cider vinegar
1 cup dark brown sugar, firmly packed
1 cup light brown sugar, firmly packed
¾ cup dark seedless raisins
2 small garlic cloves, finely minced
⅔ cup finely-chopped sweet onion, such as Vidalia
⅓ cup finely-chopped crystallized ginger
¾ teaspoon ground cinnamon
⅛ teaspoon ground cloves
1½ teaspoons dry mustard
1 teaspoon salt

Place the peaches, their juices, the vinegar and both kinds of sugar in a large nonreactive saucepan, setting the heat to medium. When mixture begins to barely bubble, remove from heat and use a potato masher to lightly mash some of the peaches – about one-third. Don't get carried away — most of the peaches should remain in chunks. Add the remainder of the ingredients, stir to combine and return to heat. Bring mixture slowly to a boil, then reduce the heat to low and simmer, uncovered, for about 1 hour, stirring occasionally. When the chutney has thickened, remove it from the heat and let it cool. Refrigerate until chilled. Chutney should be served chilled. It will keep in the refrigerator for 3-4 months. Makes about 3 cups.

The use of condiments is a trademark of Lowcountry cooking. You'll find turkey on Thanksgiving tables all over the country — but if you find a dish of relish or chutney being passed with it, you know you're in South Carolina.

The recipe here is one that I tinkered with for a while, until I hit on a version I liked. I started with the recipe in *My Mother's Southern Entertaining*, by James Villas with Martha Pearl Villas, and I ended up changing the spices around and adding an ingredient — crystallized ginger — that I saw mentioned in a number of other recipes.

Ken and I like this with pork tenderloin or chicken breasts hot off the grill.

If you're looking for the best peaches at the farmers' market, your nose knows. Give 'em a sniff – the best ones will smell wonderfully fragrant. As the farmers will tell you, though, the ones they bring to market often feel hard. That's because the peaches must be pretty firm when picked in order to survive the trip to market. Never fear — they'll ripen.

Microwave Pickles

*I was introduced to this recipe when several readers submitted it to "What's Cookin'," the Sunday recipe column that I write for **The Post and Courier**. Pickles don't get much easier than this!*

½ cup white vinegar
½ cup sugar
½ teaspoon salt
½ teaspoon mustard seed
½ teaspoon celery seed
1 teaspoon turmeric
2 large cucumbers, sliced thin
1 medium onion, sliced thin

Mix all ingredients except cucumbers and onions in a glass microwave-safe dish. Add sliced cucumbers and onions. Stir. Cover the dish and microwave on high for 7 minutes – no longer. Remove the cover, stir, then let the mixture stand undisturbed for 30 minutes. Place the pickles in jars and refrigerate. Makes 2 pints.

Palmetto Pesto for Pasta

2 large or 3 small cloves garlic, peeled
½ teaspoon salt
¼ cup pine nuts, lightly toasted and cooled
¼ cup pecan pieces, lightly toasted and cooled
4 cups loosely-packed fresh basil leaves
½ cup top-quality olive oil
¾-1 cup freshly-grated Parmesan cheese

In a food processor, using the blade attachment, place the garlic cloves, salt, pine nuts and pecans. Pulse on low for about 10 seconds. Add basil leaves and pulse for 10-15 seconds, scraping down the sides of the work bowl as needed. With the processor running, slowly pour in the olive oil. Add the Parmesan and pulse again briefly to blend. Makes about 1 cup pesto, enough for 1 pound pasta, cooked.

Basil is a favorite herb in the kitchen gardens kept by so many Lowcountry cooks. Genova basil is a traditional variety for the classic Italian sauce called pesto.

Most pesto uses pine nuts, but I give mine a Palmetto State touch by using pecans as well. I like the texture they add to the finished sauce.

Whenever I make a batch of pesto during the summer, I double the recipe — half to use right away and half to freeze for the winter months, when I crave a taste of my summer herb garden.

If you grow flat-leaf parsley, you can stretch your basil supply a bit by using 1 cup parsley leaves with 3 cups basil leaves in this recipe.

Eggplant Parmesan

True, this is an Italian dish – but South Carolina produce markets offer some terrific eggplant every summer, and this is a delicious way to put them to use.

Edie got this recipe from her friend Lidie Peery and has made only a few changes over the years.

You can make this recipe in two 8x8-inch pans; each one will serve a family of four. Edie often doubles the recipe and puts four 8x8 pans of the casserole (uncooked) in the freezer to have on hand for quick suppers.

1 large eggplant
1 teaspoon salt
½ cup plus 1 tablespoon butter, divided
Olive oil, as needed
1 medium sweet onion
1 green bell pepper
1½ pounds ground chuck
1 (28-ounce) can crushed tomatoes, with juices
1 (6-ounce) can tomato paste
½ teaspoon each dried oregano, basil, marjoram
Salt and pepper, to taste
3 large eggs, beaten
¾ cup bread crumbs, plus more if needed
2-3 cups shredded mozzarella cheese
1½ cups freshly-grated Parmesan cheese

Cut the eggplant in ¼-inch-thick slices. Sprinkle with salt and let stand for 1 hour on paper towels. In a skillet, melt 1 tablespoon of the butter. Add the onion, green pepper and meat; cook until the meat is browned, then drain. Add the tomatoes, tomato paste, oregano, basil, marjoram, salt and pepper. Simmer for 30 minutes. Dip the eggplant slices in the beaten eggs, then in the crumbs. Place the ½ cup butter and a little olive oil in a skillet and fry the eggplant until golden on both sides. Set eggplant slices on paper towels to drain. In a 13x9x2-inch baking dish, layer ingredients as follows: one-third of the meat sauce; half the eggplant slices; half the mozzarella; one-quarter of the Parmesan; another one-third of the meat sauce; remaining eggplant slices; remaining mozzarella; one-quarter of the Parmesan. Put the rest of the meat sauce on top, then the remaining Parmesan. Bake at 350 degrees for 30-35 minutes. Makes about 6 servings.

Pork Tenderloin with Fresh Peaches and Rosemary

1½ pounds pork tenderloin, cut crosswise into 1-inch-thick slices
4 tablespoons butter, divided
Salt and freshly-ground black pepper, to taste
4 medium peaches, peeled, each one cut into 8 wedges
4 shallots, minced
1 tablespoon finely-chopped fresh rosemary
½ cup peach nectar
4 tablespoons fresh lemon juice
1 cup chicken broth
½ cup whipping cream

Some herbs can't stand the intense heat of a South Carolina summer, but rosemary positively flourishes in it. With a pork tenderloin and some fresh peaches, it contributes to a wonderful summer supper. This is another recipe with an unknown source.

Flatten the pork slices to about ¼-inch thickness between sheets of plastic wrap. In a large, heavy skillet, heat 2 tablespoons butter over medium-high heat. Pat the pork slices dry; season with salt and pepper. Sauté the pork in the butter for 4 minutes, turning once, or until just cooked through. Transfer the pork to a platter; cover and keep warm. To the same skillet in which you cooked the pork, add the remaining butter. Add the peach wedges and cook, covered, over medium-high heat for 2 minutes, or until just tender. Transfer the peaches to the platter, placing them alongside the pork; re-cover and keep warm. Add the shallots to the skillet and cook over medium heat, stirring, for 2 minutes. Add the rosemary, peach nectar and lemon juice. "Deglaze" the skillet by stirring and scraping up any browned bits of pork or peach that are stuck to the

bottom of the pan. Bring the mixture to a boil and cook, stirring occasionally, until the total amount of liquid in the pan is reduced to about ¼ cup (the rest of the liquid will evaporate as it boils). Add the chicken broth and boil the liquid until the total amount is reduced by half. Add the cream, then the pork slices and any juices that have accumulated on the platter – do not add the peaches, though. Boil the mixture, stirring and turning the pork occasionally, for 1 minute, or until the sauce thickens slightly. To serve, place the pork slices on plates, with peach slices on top or alongside. Spoon the sauce over the pork and peaches. Makes 6 servings.

Beer-Batter Fried Shrimp

8 ounces beer (your choice of brands)
1 egg, slightly beaten
1 teaspoon salt
1 teaspoon paprika
Vegetable oil, for frying
1½ pounds raw shrimp, peeled
One-quarter of one lemon
1 cup sifted all-purpose flour
(sift before measuring)

Whenever we get our hands on some big, fat shrimp, we start making plans to fry them for supper. These are just terrific. Serve them with a little tartar sauce on the side.

Set a wire rack (such as you'd use to cool cookies) over several layers of paper towels. In a mixing bowl, combine the beer, egg, salt and paprika, whisking to combine. Heat an inch or so of oil in a skillet (or, using more oil, heat the oil in a small, countertop-size fryer). The oil should be very hot. Sprinkle the shrimp with lemon juice, then coat them (several at a time) with the flour. Dip them in the batter, then add them to the hot oil. Fry for 3-4 minutes, until the batter puffs around the shrimp and turns light golden. Remove the shrimp to the wire rack to drain briefly, then serve. Makes 4 servings.

Crab Imperial

"*Imperial*" *fits in the name of this dish because it's certainly fit for a king. This longtime family favorite originally came from* **The Captain's Cookbook**, *which Dad gave Mom years ago. Mom has tinkered with it a bit over the years, and we think it's terrific. If you can get your hands on some seashell-shaped individual dishes in which to bake and serve this, the spirit of the dish is complete.*

1 pound crabmeat
2 tablespoons butter, divided
1 tablespoon all-purpose flour
½ cup milk
1 teaspoon instant minced onion
1½ teaspoons Worcestershire sauce
2-3 slices white bread, crusts cut off, bread cubed
½ cup mayonnaise
¾ teaspoon salt
Freshly-ground black pepper, to taste
½ teaspoon fresh lemon juice, or more, to taste
Paprika

Preheat the oven to 450 degrees. Pick over the crab to be sure all pieces of shell and cartilage are removed. Set the crabmeat aside. In a small saucepan over low heat, melt the butter, then slowly add the flour, stirring until the mixture is smooth. Add the milk, stirring constantly, and increase the heat to medium. Cook until the mixture thickens, then gently stir in the minced onion, Worcestershire and cubes of bread. Set the mixture aside; when it is cool, stir in the mayonnaise, salt, pepper and lemon juice. In a large pan, melt the remaining tablespoon of butter over low heat. Add the crabmeat and cook, stirring, just until golden; combine the crabmeat and the bread mixture. Spoon the mixture into a 1-quart casserole dish or individual baking dishes. Sprinkle with a bit of paprika. Bake for 12-15 minutes, or until the mixture is hot, bubbly at the edges, and golden on top. Makes 4 servings.

Jack's Favorite Crab Cakes

1 pound crabmeat, picked over to remove any traces of shell
½ cup Ritz cracker crumbs, plus more for coating the crab cakes
½ cup finely-chopped celery
½ to ¾ cup mayonnaise
Juice of one-half lemon
Salt, to taste
White, red and/or black pepper, to taste
½ teaspoon Worcestershire sauce
½ teaspoon hot English mustard paste
Canola oil and/or butter, for cooking

Some crab cakes have as much breading as they have crab, and some have more breading than crab. Not so with these. They're Dad's favorite version, and the rest of the family's, too.

Combine all ingredients in a mixing bowl, stirring to mix well. Using your hands, shape the mixture into cakes, each one about 2 inches across and ¾-inch thick. Roll in cracker crumbs and refrigerate for an hour before cooking, or wrap them individually and freeze them in a large resealable plastic bag. Cook them straight from the freezer (which will take a few extra minutes) or defrost in the refrigerator before cooking. To cook, heat a small amount of canola oil or butter, or a mixture of the two, in a skillet. Add the crab cakes and cook over medium heat until golden brown, turning once during the cooking process, approximately 10 minutes. Makes 12 crab cakes.

Shrimp and Crab in Patty Shells

When Aunt Jean built a dock on the Cooper River in 1972, we had access to just about every pleasure of summer that a child could want — swimming, shrimping, crabbing, sunbathing, sailing, watching meteor showers and fireworks shows on summer nights. It was paradise.

Changes in the harbor have redirected the shrimp and crab populations farther out in Charleston Harbor, so these days we don't catch them off the dock as often as we used to. But when we're having a run of luck, this family favorite is always near the top of the request list when supper rolls around.

"Patty shells," by the way, are what some Charlestonians call puff pastry shells.

You can use all crab or all shrimp in this recipe, if you prefer.

3 tablespoons butter or margarine
2 tablespoons all-purpose flour
1 teaspoon salt
1 teaspoon prepared mustard
¾ cup whole milk
½ teaspoon Worcestershire sauce
¼ teaspoon garlic salt
1 teaspoon fresh lemon juice
Dash of white pepper
Dash of Tabasco
2 cups fresh crabmeat
1 cup cooked, peeled shrimp, deveined
Patty shells (puff pastry shells, found in the freezer case at most supermarkets)

In the top of a double boiler over simmering water, melt the butter. Stir in the flour, salt and mustard, pressing out any lumps so that a smooth paste is formed. When the mixture barely begins to bubble, add the milk; cook over medium heat, stirring constantly, until thickened. Stir in Worcestershire, garlic salt, lemon juice, pepper and Tabasco. Stir in the crab and shrimp. Reduce the heat and cook until the shrimp are heated through, about 5 minutes. Meanwhile, warm patty shells as directed on package until they're flaky and light golden brown. To serve, spoon shrimp, crab and sauce into shells. Makes 4-6 servings.

Sautéed Flounder with Fresh Tomato, Corn and Avocado Salsa

For the salsa:

4 medium tomatoes, peeled, seeded and diced
Half of an avocado, diced
Juice of half a lime
3 green onions, sliced vertically, then chopped
Corn kernels cut from 1 ear fresh, cooked corn
4 tablespoons fresh basil, chopped
3 tablespoons fresh chives, chopped
¼ cup olive oil
2 cloves garlic, minced
4 saffron threads
¼ teaspoon honey
Dash of cumin
Salt and freshly-ground black pepper, to taste

For the fish:

6 flounder fillets, about 6 ounces each, skinned
1 tablespoon olive oil
1 tablespoon butter
Chopped fresh basil, for garnish

*This recipe comes from Holly Herrick, a restaurant reviewer for **The Post and Courier**. Holly loves to fish, and it really shows in the care and skill with which she prepares her catch.*

Flounder is delicate, so it's easier to handle in a sauté pan than on the grill, Holly says. However, it is "grillable" if you leave the skin on, brush the fish well with oil, and keep the heat high.

With some home-grown tomatoes and sweet Silver Queen corn, this makes an outstanding summer supper.

To make the salsa: Gently combine all of the salsa ingredients in a medium bowl, folding with a wooden spoon to prevent breaking the avocados. Check seasonings and adjust if needed. Refrigerate and chill up to six hours, then bring to room temperature before serving.

To make the fish, rinse the fillets carefully and remove any bones you see. Pat dry. Heat a large, nonstick skillet over medium-high heat. Add the butter and oil. Season the fish on both sides. Place the fillets in a single layer in the pan (you might have to work in batches). Cook about 2 minutes on each side, flipping only once. When the fish are golden brown and opaque in the center, serve immediately with a generous helping of salsa and a sprinkling of fresh basil. Makes 6 servings.

Tuna with Thai Marinade

½ cup sesame oil
1 cup soy sauce
½ cup fresh lime juice
¼ cup sake or sherry
2 tablespoons finely-minced fresh garlic
2 tablespoons chopped fresh ginger
1 to 3 tablespoons crushed red pepper flakes
(adjust heat level to your taste)
4 thick fresh tuna steaks, about 6 ounces each
Toasted sesame seeds

Fresh tuna is a real prize for all the fishermen I know in the Lowcountry — and it's among the easiest kinds of fish to grill because the steaks are firm and easy to handle. This marinade — source unknown — has made the rounds among my sister Edie and her friends.

In a small bowl, combine all the ingredients except the tuna and sesame seeds; stir with a whisk to combine. Place the tuna steaks in a glass baking dish, then pour the marinade on top. Marinate at room temperature for 30 minutes — no longer — turning the steaks once halfway through. Grill to your preferred degree of doneness (or pan-sear in a little olive oil). Sprinkle on some sesame seeds just before serving. Makes 4 servings.

It only takes a minute to toast sesame seeds, which really enhances their flavor. You can toast them in a dry pan on top of the stove, or on a baking sheet in your toaster oven. However you do it, watch them closely — they can burn awfully fast.

yummy Marinade for Chicken! Add to a Asian Salad (mixed greens, green onion, mand. oranges, celery, Chinese noodle)

Creamy Shrimp and Rice Casserole

The small shrimp of late summer are tender and bite-size and perfect for this casserole. It can be prepared the night before or the morning of sewing, and stored, covered, in the refrigerator until it's time to cook.

This recipe came to us from longtime family friend Marsha Paulling.

3 cups cooked, peeled, small shrimp (if the shrimp are large, cut them into smaller bite-size pieces)
2 cups cooked rice
1 small sweet onion, diced
1 cup diced celery
4 hard-boiled eggs, peeled and chopped
2 (10-ounce) cans cream of shrimp soup
¾ cup mayonnaise
1 teaspoon fresh lemon juice
½ cup water
1 (3-ounce) package sliced almonds
2 tablespoons butter, melted
1 cup dry bread crumbs

Preheat the oven to 350 degrees. In a large mixing bowl, stir together all the ingredients except for the butter and bread crumbs. Spread mixture into a 13x9-inch baking dish. (If you want to refrigerate it now for baking later, do so at this point.) When ready to cook, combine the melted butter and bread crumbs. Sprinkle the buttered crumbs on top of the casserole. Bake for 25-30 minutes, until hot and bubbly. Makes 4-6 servings.

You can substitute chicken for the shrimp in this recipe. Instead of the shrimp, use 3 cups diced, cooked chicken; instead of the shrimp soup, use 2 cans cream of chicken soup; use 1 cup of mayonnaise, and omit the lemon juice and water. Bake at 350 degrees for 40-45 minutes.

Summer Peach Crunch

3 cups sliced fresh peaches
1 tablespoon fresh lemon juice
1 cup self-rising flour
1 cup sugar
1 large egg
6 tablespoons butter

Preheat the oven to 375 degrees. Place the sliced peaches in a 1½ quart baking dish. Sprinkle the lemon juice over the peaches and stir gently to coat. In a small bowl, combine the flour, sugar and egg. Stir until the egg is broken up and the mixture is somewhat lumpy (it will be very dry). Spread the mixture on top of the peaches. Melt the butter and pour it over the top of the flour mixture; do not stir. Bake in the middle of the oven for 25-30 minutes. Serve warm. Makes about 6 servings.

I can't remember a time when my family didn't make Peach Crunch. It has a special place in my heart because my mother clipped the recipe out of the newspaper's "Loved and Lost" column in the late 1960s or early '70s, when Charlotte Walker was the food editor. "Loved and Lost" was the paper's first recipe exchange column. When Mrs. Walker retired, the name retired with her — the two are inseparable. The column I write today, "What's Cookin'," owes everything to "Loved and Lost."

Make this cobbler-style dessert with summer's best, juiciest peaches. If you crave it during the winter but didn't freeze any peaches when they were in season, you can use frozen peaches. Serve this with a scoop of vanilla ice cream or a dollop of whipped cream for an extra-decadent treat.

A-B-C Banana Pudding

**1 large box instant vanilla pudding
1 large (8- or 12-ounce) tub prepared whipped topping, thawed
1 box vanilla wafers
6-8 ripe bananas, sliced about ¼-inch-thick**

Prepare the pudding according to package directions. Fold in about three-quarters of the whipped topping. In a deep serving bowl, layer the ingredients in this order: vanilla wafers, half the banana slices, half the pudding mixture. Repeat layers in the same order. Spread the remaining whipped topping over the top. Cover and chill thoroughly for several hours before serving. Makes 8-10 good-size servings.

My mother-in-law, Anna Burger, whipped up this dessert one summer when she came to visit Ken and I and his three children, then teenagers, were spending a week in a beach house on the Isle of Palms, just outside Charleston. As usual, a bunch of bananas had gotten super-ripe before we were able to use them all, so Anna suggested this as a good way to use them. We can't recall where the recipe originally came from, but we renamed it A-B-C Banana Pudding — not just because it's easy, but because those are first initials of Ken's now grownup children, Allyson, Brent and Courtney.

Perfect Peach Pie

6 cups sliced fresh peaches
1¾ cups sugar
¼ cup all-purpose flour
½ teaspoon ground nutmeg
¾ teaspoon vanilla extract
3 tablespoons butter
Pastry for a double crust 9-inch pie

Becky Rakestraw, a friend of my sister Edie's, shared this recipe. A homemade pie crust is always divine, but prepared pastry sheets from the freezer case at the grocery store work just fine — and make things cool and easy on a summer day.

Preheat the oven to 425 degrees. Combine the peaches, sugar, flour and nutmeg in a saucepan. Set aside for about 30-45 minutes, or until a syrup begins to form. Place the saucepan over medium-high heat and bring the peach mixture to a boil; reduce the heat to low and cook for 10 minutes, or until the peaches are tender, stirring often. Remove the pan from the heat; add the vanilla and butter, stirring until well-combined. Put half of the pastry in a 9-inch pie plate. Fill with the peach filling. Cover the pie with the remaining pastry (or, cut the pastry into strips and make a lattice on top of the pie). Bake at 425 degrees for 10 minutes. Reduce the heat to 350 degrees and bake 30 minutes more, or until the crust is browned. Makes 8 servings.

Truth be told, South Carolina deserves the name "Peach State" more than Georgia does — we're second only to California in the annual production of these gems, many of which come from Upstate towns such as Gaffney.

Fresh Peach Ice Cream

"Divine" is the word for ice cream made from fresh South Carolina peaches. The Upstate is our peachiest region, but these favorite fruits are grown in many parts of the Palmetto State.

You'll need to mash the peaches for this ice cream; serve slices of fresh peach alongside for chunks of extra sweetness.

1½ cups whole milk
1 large egg
⅓ cup sugar
1 teaspoon vanilla extract
1 cup whipping cream
1½ cups mashed fresh peaches with juices

In a saucepan over medium-low heat, warm the milk just until it's hot — do not let it boil or scald. While the milk is heating, beat the egg and sugar together in a bowl until combined. When the milk is hot, pour a small amount of it slowly into the beaten egg, stirring so the milk warms the egg gradually. Then, pour the egg mixture slowly into the hot milk in the saucepan. Cook over low heat, stirring constantly, until the custard thickens slightly (it should coat the back of a spoon). Immediately remove the pan from the heat and add the vanilla. Pour the custard into a bowl, cover, and refrigerate it until it's thoroughly chilled. To make the ice cream, remove the custard from the refrigerator and stir in the whipping cream. Pour the mixture into the ice cream maker and, when it just begins to get firm, add the peaches. Continue churning according to the ice cream maker's instructions. Makes 1 quart.

Jack's Birthday Ice Cream

2 cups whole milk
2 large eggs
⅓-½ cup sugar
1 tablespoon cornstarch dissolved in a little water
1 cup miniature marshmallows
2 teaspoons vanilla extract
½ pint whipping cream
1 (8-ounce) can crushed pineapple, chilled and drained
1 (10-ounce) jar maraschino cherries, chilled and drained
¼ cup chopped pecans (optional)
Juice of half a lemon

In a saucepan, warm the milk until it's just hot — do not let it boil or scald. While the milk is heating, beat the eggs and sugar together in a bowl until combined. When the milk is hot, pour a small amount of it (maybe ½ cup) slowly into the beaten eggs, stirring so the milk warms the eggs gradually. Then, pour the egg mixture slowly into the hot milk in the saucepan. Add the dissolved cornstarch and cook the whole thing slowly over low heat, just until the custard thickens slightly (it should coat the back of a spoon). Immediately remove the custard from the heat and, while it's still hot, stir in the marshmallows and vanilla. Pour the mixture into a bowl, cover it, and refrigerate it until the custard is thoroughly chilled. To make the ice cream, remove the custard from the refrigerator and stir in the whipping cream. Pour the custard into your ice cream freezer and (either now or after the ice

When I was a girl, we had a pale yellow, electric ice cream churn – the kind that took bags and bags of ice and lots of rock salt around the sides to churn the custard into cream. One of my happy memories is of being small enough to sit on the kitchen counter beside the churn and pour in the rock salt when Mom gave me a nod. When the ice cream was finally ready, we all wanted to be the lucky one who got to lick the dasher.

When the handy 1-quart ice cream makers came out, Mom recalculated the recipe to fit the smaller capacity of the cannister. While I love the convenience of the neat new churns, the dasher is awfully small compared to the old-fashioned one!

cream has begun to set) stir in the chilled pineapple with its juice, the cherries, nuts and lemon juice. Churn the ice cream according to the ice cream maker's instructions. Makes 1 quart.

Mom says she's found that adding the cornstarch to the custard seems to give the ice cream a better texture for holding together all the fruit and nuts. Another thickener comes from the marshmallows, which tend to melt slightly in the warm custard.

Lemon Ice Cream

*F*resh fruit —
especially sliced peaches
and strawberries — are
delicious with this
super-cooling ice cream.
It's wonderfully creamy,
but also has that lemon
tartness to balance its rich
flavor. This recipe is made
for a 1-quart churn.

1 cup whole milk
1 scant cup sugar
Juice of 2 lemons
Finely-grated rind (zest) of 1 lemon
1 cup whipping cream

In a saucepan over medium-low heat, warm the milk just until it's hot — do not let it boil or scald. When it's hot, add the sugar, stirring until it's dissolved. Remove the pan from the heat, let the mixture cool, then cover and refrigerate it until it's thoroughly chilled. To make the ice cream, stir the lemon juice, zest and whipping cream into the milk mixture. Freeze according to the ice cream maker's instructions. Makes 1 quart.

Peach-A-Berry Cobbler

1 tablespoon cornstarch
¼ cup brown sugar
½ cup cold water
2 cups sliced fresh peaches, sprinkled lightly with sugar
1 cup fresh blueberries
5 tablespoons butter, softened
1 tablespoon fresh lemon juice
1 cup sifted all-purpose flour
(sift before measuring)
½ cup plus 2 tablespoons sugar, divided
1½ teaspoons baking powder
½ teaspoon salt
½ cup milk
4 tablespoons butter, softened
¼ teaspoon ground nutmeg

Preheat the oven to 350 degrees. In a saucepan, combine the cornstarch, brown sugar and cold water. Add the peaches and blueberries and cook, stirring, over medium heat until the mixture thickens. Stir in 1 tablespoon of the butter and the lemon juice. Pour the mixture into an 8¼ x 1¾-inch round ovenware cake dish. Sift the flour, ½ cup of the sugar, the baking powder and salt into a mixing bowl. Add the milk and the remainder of the softened butter all at once and beat with an electric mixer until smooth. Pour this over the fruit mixture. Sprinkle the remaining 2 tablespoons sugar and the ground nutmeg on top. Bake the cobbler for 30 minutes. Makes 6-8 servings.

Betty and Cameron Burn have lived across the street from my parents for more than 50 years. They have the same anniversary that Mom and Dad do, and their driveway basketball court was a neighborhood hangout in the '60s and '70s. I got a reputation as a secret weapon because, when I was so little that people would forget I was playing, I'd stand right under the basket, overlooked, and wait until my teammates threw me the ball. Before anyone remembered I was there, I'd shoot – and I was so close to the basket that I usually scored.

This recipe from Mrs. Burn uses fresh peaches and another favorite South Carolina fruit – blueberries. I like it with fresh cream or vanilla ice cream.

Fall

Fall

*M*y mother held my small hand, leading me down the paths between the pumpkins that seemed so big and so orange I thought the moon had laid eggs overnight.

Such are the memories of youth, when the first frost bites gently on your nose, then spreads itself out over meadows like a sheet of crystallized glass. When you zip your windbreaker all the way up, only to find the collar does not cover your ears. You shiver, but it only reminds you that your breakfast of hot cakes and crisp bacon has burned away as the promise of grilled cheese sandwiches calls you back to the table for lunch.

These are the chilly days when cocoa finds its way out of the back of the cupboard and onto the stove, where it's mixed with warm milk and melts its way into your heart.

While walking along paths, crunching the leaves beneath your feet, you are always reminded of autumn nights at high school football games and Saturday mornings down at the farmer's market. You watch pecans falling noisily from the trees, knowing they are destined for a Thanksgiving pie.

This is the season when good cooks spread a little brown sugar on almost anything to give it a generous glaze and the smell of cinnamon drifts from the kitchen into the hallways, where it lingers and saturates the soul.

I cannot recall an October weekend when the

small country roads were not filled with pickup trucks driven by bearded men headed for deer stands deep in the swamps. Or afternoons when their convoys rolled back from the hunt with trophy bucks draped across their fenders.

On other mornings, you might awaken to the sound of trailer hitches snapping into place and jon boats bouncing down dirt roads that ran like riverlets to the sea. As a small boy I watched old men slip their crafts into the brackish waters, fanning out their nets like umbrellas that splashed onto the water and sank silently to where the bottom-feeders dwell. Once hauled aboard, shrimp the size of summer sausages wriggled in the nets before they were shelled and served up in a Frogmore stew for supper.

These are the days that deserve to be captured in smells and tastes and lifelong memories before winter comes along and quiets the landscape.

Ken

Grandmother's Nut Bread

1 cup chopped pecans
2 cups all-purpose flour
1 teaspoon baking powder
Pinch of salt
1 cup sugar
1 large egg
1 cup milk
1 walnut-size piece of butter, softened

Preheat the oven to 350 degrees. Grease a loaf pan (about 9 inches by 5 inches). Place the pecans in a small bowl and sprinkle a teaspoon or so of the flour (from the 2 cups) on top. Stir the nuts around so they're lightly dusted. (This will help suspend the nuts in the batter so they don't all sink to the bottom.) Put the remaining flour, baking powder, salt and sugar in a mixing bowl; whisk to combine. Add the egg, milk and butter; whisk again to combine. Stir in the floured nuts. Pour the batter into the prepared pan and bake the bread for 50 minutes-1 hour, until the top is golden. Cool 15 minutes in the pan on a wire rack, then remove the bread from the pan and slice with a serrated knife. Serve warm with butter. Makes 8-10 slices.

This recipe, like many found on the browning pages of our old family recipe book, is hand-written, with a list of ingredients and a baking time and temperature – but no instructions otherwise. Whenever I look at the little book, I'm amazed at all the cakes, candies, breads and more that include no specifics on how to combine ingredients. I guess a knowledge of the basic techniques was just assumed. Personally, I'll take all the instruction I can get!

The first time I made this sweet, nutty bread, I was winging it, and it turned out well. I felt like I was connecting with all the good cooks in my past when I measured out that "walnut-size piece of butter." While the ingredient list is Grandmother's (actually, she was my mother's grand-mother, so she's my great-grandmother), the directions are mine.

This dense bread is best served fresh out of the oven – with some more of that good old butter.

Plump Pumpkin Muffins

I really know it's fall when the sugar pumpkins arrive at the farmers' markets. These aren't the big carving pumpkins that we use to make jack-o'lanterns; they're smaller, often smoother, deeply orange-colored pumpkins that are better for cooking because they're far less watery and stringy.

You can roast your own pumpkin for these muffins – the recipe is from Edie's collection – or you can use canned pumpkin with terrific results. Pumpkin, unlike many vegetables, doesn't lose anything in the transition from fresh to canned.

2 cups all-purpose flour
1 tablespoon baking powder
½ teaspoon salt
½ teaspoon ginger
¼ teaspoon nutmeg
1 teaspoon cinnamon
⅛ teaspoon ground cloves
⅔ cup sugar
1 large egg, beaten
1 cup sour cream
2 to 3 tablespoons sweet orange marmalade
⅓ cup vegetable oil
1 cup pumpkin purée (canned or fresh)

Sift the flour, baking powder, salt, ginger, nutmeg, cinnamon, cloves and sugar into a large bowl. In another bowl, stir together the egg, sour cream, orange marmalade, oil and pumpkin. Add this to the flour mixture, stirring just until moistened (the batter may be lumpy). Line a regular-size muffin tin with muffin cups. Spray the liners lightly with nonstick cooking spray, then spoon in the batter, filling each cup full. Bake for 18-20 minutes, or until the muffins are golden.

To roast fresh pumpkin, cut the pumpkin in half, scoop out the seeds and stringy flesh, and place the pumpkin cut-side down on a baking sheet. Roast at 425 degrees for about 1 hour, or until the flesh is soft. After that, just peel off the skin and puree the flesh. (It freezes well, if you want to stock up.) A 3 to 5 pound pumpkin will yield approximately 1 cup of pumpkin purée.

Brown Sugar-Cream Cheese Muffins

½ cup light brown sugar, firmly packed
⅓ cup butter, softened
1 (3-ounce) package cream cheese, softened
⅔ cup milk
1 large egg
1 teaspoon maple extract or vanilla extract
1 cup old-fashioned (not instant) oats, uncooked
½ cup all-purpose flour
⅓ cup whole wheat flour
1 tablespoon baking powder
½ teaspoon salt
1 cup chopped pecans, divided

This recipe came from the newspaper some years ago, and unfortunately I didn't clip out the origin when I clipped out the recipe. The muffins freeze well – if there are any left over after everybody digs in.

Preheat the oven to 400 degrees. Grease only the bottoms of 12 standard muffin cups, or line the muffin tin with paper baking cups. In a medium bowl, beat the brown sugar, butter and cream cheese with an electric mixer until light and fluffy. Add the milk, egg and extract, mixing well. In another bowl, combine the oats, both kinds of flour, the baking powder and salt; whisk to combine. Add this and ½ cup of the pecans to the sugar-butter mixture, stirring just until the dry ingredients are moistened. Spoon the batter into the muffin cups, filling each one three-quarters full. Sprinkle the remaining chopped pecans on the tops. Bake for 18-22 minutes, or until the muffins are golden brown. Serve slightly warm. Makes 1 dozen muffins.

To freeze, wrap individual muffins securely in plastic wrap, then place in a resealable zipper-top bag and freeze. To reheat muffins directly from the freezer, unwrap as many as you need and microwave them on high for 40-45 seconds per muffin.

Crispy Che

Crispy rice cereal adds a nice touch to these cheesy appetizers, and fat fall pecans top them off perfectly. You can crank the heat level up or down as you choose.

These little crackers are great for holiday parties or gift-giving.

**2 cups shredded shar
2 sticks butter, at ro
Ground red pepper (
½ teaspoon dry mustard
1½ cups all-purpose flour
2 cups crisped rice cereal
Pecan halves**

Preheat the oven to 350 degrees. Combine the cheese and butter in a large mixing bowl. Using an electric mixer, beat at medium speed until well combined. Add the red pepper and mustard. Slowly beat in the flour, mixing until blended. Stir in the cereal. Form the dough into 1-inch balls and place the balls on an ungreased cookie sheet about 2 inches apart. Lightly press the crackers to flatten, using the bottom of a glass (dusted lightly with extra flour, if needed, to keep it from sticking to the dough). Press a pecan half into the center of each cracker. Bake the crackers for 10-12 minutes. Cool for 1 minute on the cookie sheet, then remove cookies to a wire rack to finish cooling. Store in an airtight container. Makes approximately 5 dozen crackers.

Nutty Cheese Log

8 ounces sharp or extra-sharp cheddar cheese, grated
4 ounces cream cheese, softened
Dash of Tabasco sauce
1 clove garlic, grated
¼ teaspoon salt
1½ teaspoons Worcestershire sauce
Juice of one-quarter of a small lemon
¾ to 1 cup chopped pecans

If you're in the market for an easy appetizer, this is the ticket. It's great for parties because you can make it ahead of time, and it also makes a thoughtful hostess gift.

Combine all the ingredients except the pecans in a mixing bowl and blend well, using an electric mixer. Shape the mixture into a log and roll it in the chopped pecans. Sprinkle with paprika. Refrigerate until the log is firm. Serve with assorted crackers. Makes 1 log, about 8 inches long.

Andy's Maple-Glazed Pecans

*A*ndy Felts, The *Post and Courier's* wine columnist, passed along this recipe for glazed pecans, which he often prepares as gifts for the holidays.

4 cups pecan halves
½ cup pure maple syrup
1½ tablespoons heavy cream
1½ tablespoons Grand Marnier (orange liqueur)
¼ teaspoon salt
¼ teaspoon cinnamon

Preheat the oven to 350 degrees. Place the pecan halves on a cookie sheet and bake for 10-12 minutes, until the nuts are fragrant. Meanwhile, combine syrup, cream and Grand Marnier in a saucepan large enough to hold the nuts. Bring mixture to a boil and boil for 2 minutes. Remove from heat and stir in the salt and cinnamon. Add the warm pecans, stirring to coat them with the glaze. Place the pecan halves back on the cookie sheet, keeping them relatively separated, and return to the oven. Bake for 10 minutes. Place the cookie sheet on a wire rack until the nuts cool; if necessary, break apart any that have stuck together. Makes 4 cups.

Simply Salted Nuts

4 cups pecan halves
½-1 stick butter
Salt, to taste

Preheat the oven to 300 degrees. Spread the nuts in a single layer on a large, flat pan, such as a cookie sheet or jelly roll pan. Cut ½ stick butter into small chunks and dot them on top of the nuts. Place the nuts in the oven on a middle rack. After 10 minutes, remove the pan from the oven and stir the nuts so the butter (which will have melted) coats them. Sprinkle salt over the nuts and return the pan to the oven. After 6 minutes, remove the pan, stir the nuts, and add more butter and/or salt as you wish. Return the pan to the oven and roast the nuts for 6 minutes more. Remove the pan from the oven once more. Stir the nuts, adding more butter and/or salt as desired. Return the pan to the oven one final time and bake for 6 minutes. Remove the pan from the oven and place it on a wire rack to cool for several minutes. Turn the nuts out onto paper towels and let them cool completely. Transfer them to an airtight container for storage. Makes 4 cups.

Every fall I get Ken to stop by the Golden Kernel Pecan Co. in Cameron, S.C., when he's on his way home from a University of South Carolina football game in Columbia. He always picks up a quantity of beautiful, fat pecan halves for me to salt — not just for the family, but also for gifts or to take to parties.

This recipe is pretty simple and straightforward, but that's what we like about it. When you've got rich roasted pecans as your main ingredient, what more do you really need anyway?

You can vary the amount of butter and salt up or down, according to your taste. I've never used margarine for these. Only butter will do!

Fall Fruit Chutney

Tart apples and sweet pears team up in this chutney, which is spiced up with cinnamon, cloves and crystallized ginger. A few spoonfuls of this will turn a run-of-the-mill pork chop or chicken breast into something special.

This is another recipe of unknown origin, from deep in the family files.

3 cups diced tart apples (about 1 pound apples)
5 cups diced, firm, ripe pears (about 2 pounds)
½ cup seedless raisins
1 large onion, chopped fairly small
⅓ cup finely-chopped crystallized ginger
1 cup firmly-packed light brown sugar
½ teaspoon ground cinnamon
¼ teaspoon ground cloves
1 teaspoon salt
1 cup apple cider vinegar

Combine all ingredients except the vinegar in a large, deep pot. Stir gently to combine. Add the vinegar and stir again. Bring the mixture to a boil over medium-high heat, stirring occasionally. Reduce the heat to a simmer and cook the chutney, uncovered, for 90 minutes, or until thickened. Cool to room temperature, then ladle the chutney into jars and store them in the refrigerator. Makes 5 half-pints.

Emma Law's Cranberry Sauce

1¾ cups sugar
4 tablespoons frozen orange juice concentrate, thawed (do not dilute)
¾ cup dry white wine
1 (12-ounce) bag fresh cranberries

Combine the sugar, orange juice concentrate and wine in a 4- to 5-quart saucepan. Cook over low heat until the sugar dissolves, stirring constantly, about 5-7 minutes. Add the cranberries and bring the mixture to a boil. Cook over medium-low heat for 7-10 minutes, or until the berries pop open, stirring frequently. Remove from the heat, cool to room temperature, then pour into a container with a tight-fitting lid. Chill for several hours before using (the sauce will thicken when it chills). Keeps well in the refrigerator for several weeks. Makes 2½ to 3 cups.

This is our staple cranberry sauce for Thanksgiving turkey, but it's good all through the fall and winter with pork and chicken, simply prepared.

Who's Emma Law? I have no idea. No one in our family knows who this lady is, or was, but we certainly are fond of her cranberry sauce. It wouldn't be Thanksgiving without a pretty bowl of it on the dining room table.

This recipe came into the family via Barbara Blair, the mother of Edie's husband, Andy. She clipped it out of a newspaper many years ago. Emma Law's name was on the recipe then — and it still is.

If you're looking for a little holiday treat to share with a neighbor, friend, teacher, etc., consider making and sharing a jar of this chunky sauce.

Sherried Fruit

Turkey and ham are wonderful foils for this hot baked fruit dish. It makes a pretty addition to a holiday dinner table and, because it's sweet and rich, it goes a long way.

You can assemble this dish the day before you need it, refrigerate it, and bake it right before serving.

1 (20-ounce) can pineapple slices
1 (15¼ ounce) can sliced peaches
1 (20-ounce) can apple slices (rings)
1 (15¼ ounce) can sliced apricots
1 (10-ounce) jar maraschino cherries
1 stick butter
½ cup brown sugar
1 tablespoon all-purpose flour
1 cup sherry

Preheat the oven to 325 degrees. Drain the juices from all the cans of fruit. Cut the pineapple, peaches and apple slices into bite-size pieces. Arrange all of the fruit in 13x9x2-inch baking dish. In a small saucepan, melt the butter, then stir in the brown sugar and flour. Add the sherry. Pour this sauce over the fruit. Bake for 15-20 minutes, or until the dish is hot and bubbly. Makes 12-14 servings.

Hot Curried Fruit

1 (8 to 8½ ounce) can pear halves
1 (8 to 8½ ounce) can apricot halves
1 (8 to 8½ ounce) can sliced peaches
1 (8 to 8½ ounce) can pineapple chunks
Half of a 14-ounce jar apple rings, cut in half
1½ teaspoons cornstarch
½ teaspoon curry powder
½ cup sugar (white or light brown)
2 tablespoons butter

This tasty side dish can be assembled ahead of time and stored in the refrigerator until you're ready to bake it, or you can bake it in the morning and place it in the refrigerator, then reheat it later in the day for serving.

Preheat the oven to 325 degrees. Drain the juice from all the cans of fruit, saving the juices in one large bowl (save just half of the juice from the can of apple rings). Arrange the fruit in an 8-inch square casserole dish. Place ½ cup of the reserved fruit juices in a small saucepan. Add the cornstarch and stir to dissolve it. Add the curry powder, sugar and butter to the pan and bring to a simmer; cook until the mixture begins to thicken, then pour it (while hot) over the fruit. Cover the baking dish with foil and bake the fruit for 15-20 minutes, until it's very bubbly and hot. Serve warm. Makes 4 servings.

Baked Potato Corn Soup

I f ever a soup could be a main dish, this is it. It's very rich and creamy and filling – a meal in a bowl on a cool fall day. The recipe is the result of some minor tinkering with a recipe that appeared in a 1991 Southern Living magazine collection. The most significant change I made was adding fresh corn kernels.

4 large baking potatoes
1 stick butter
⅔ cup all-purpose flour
6 cups milk (or more, for desired consistency)
2 cups fresh corn kernels
Salt and white pepper, to taste
¾ cup finely-chopped onion
10 slices bacon, cooked and crumbled, divided
1¼ cups shredded sharp cheddar cheese, divided
8 ounces sour cream
Snipped fresh chives (optional garnish)

Preheat the oven to 400 degrees. Wash the potatoes, pierce each one with the tines of a fork, and bake them for about 1 hour, or until cooked through. Let them cool completely, then cut them in half lengthwise and scoop out the pulp. (Discard the skins.) In a heavy saucepan set over low heat, melt the butter. Add the flour, stirring to make a smooth, lump-free mixture. Cook for 1 minute, stirring constantly. Slowly add 6 cups of milk; cook over medium heat, stirring constantly, until the mixture begins to thicken. Add the potato pulp, corn kernels, salt, pepper, onion, half of the crumbled bacon, and ¾ cup of the cheese. Cook until heated through. Stir in the sour cream. If you want a soup that's not so thick, add more milk. Serve the soup at once, sprinkling the remaining bacon and cheese on top. Add a sprinkle of snipped fresh chives if desired. Makes 8-10 servings.

's

n Soup

97

k beans

vater

chicken stock

1 onion, chopped
3 cloves garlic, minced
1 carrot, chopped
1 rib celery, chopped
1 tablespoon olive oil
1½ to 2 teaspoons cumin
1 teaspoon coriander
½ cup freshly-squeezed orange juice
Sections of 2 oranges
2 tablespoons dry sherry
½ teaspoon freshly-ground black pepper
¼ teaspoon ground red pepper
Juice of 1 lemon
Salt, to taste
Sour cream or plain yogurt, as a garnish
Finely chopped onion, as a garnish

lace a cruet of wine vinegar on the table when you're serving this soup; it can add a nice kick.

If you like a smoother soup, you can purée some of the cooked beans, adding them back to the pot to heat through before serving.

In a large pot, soak the beans in the water for 8-12 hours; drain off the liquid. Return the beans to the pot and add 3½ cups of the chicken stock. Bring to a boil over medium heat. Cover the pot and reduce the heat to medium-low. In a skillet, sauté the onion, garlic, carrot and celery in the olive oil until the onions become clear. Add the cumin and coriander, and a little bit of water – just enough that the vegetables will steam. Cook for several minutes, or until the vegetables are soft. Add the vegetables to the beans, then add the orange juice, orange sections, sherry, black pepper, red pepper, lemon juice and salt; stir gently. Simmer for 1½ to 2 hours, or until the beans are tender, stirring occasionally and adding more chicken stock or water if needed. To serve, ladle the soup into bowls and garnish with sour cream or plain yogurt, plus a sprinkle of finely-chopped onion. Makes 6 servings.

Gingered Carrot Soup

resh ginger and curry are wonderful additions to this carrot soup. We got the recipe from a women's magazine years ago. It's delicious warm or cold and would make a nice intro to Thanksgiving dinner.

¼ cup olive oil
2 cups chopped sweet onion
2 teaspoons minced garlic
2 teaspoons minced fresh ginger root
2 pounds carrots, coarsely chopped (to make about 5½ cups)
2 teaspoons curry powder
Salt and freshly ground black pepper, to taste
10 cups chicken broth
Snipped fresh chives (for a garnish)

In a 5- to 6-quart Dutch oven, heat the oil, then add the onions and cook about 10 minutes over low heat, until the onions are translucent. Stir in the garlic, ginger, carrots, curry powder, salt and pepper. Add the broth and bring to a boil, then reduce the heat, cover and simmer for 30-35 minutes, or until the carrots are tender. Cool the soup to room temperature, then purée it (in batches, if necessary) in a food processor or blender. To serve warm, reheat the soup and serve garnished with chives. To serve cold, chill the soup 6 hours or more. Makes 6-8 servings.

Hunter's Rice Casserole

4 tablespoons butter, divided
1½ cups uncooked, long-grain white rice
Half of a large onion, cut in small dice
8-10 ounces fresh mushrooms, such as cremini,
washed and stemmed
2 (10½ ounce) cans beef broth
1 cup water
Salt and freshly ground black pepper, to taste

This easy side-dish is great with game, hence its name. Try it with doves, duck or venison; it's also nice with chicken.

Preheat the oven to 350 degrees. In a skillet, melt 3 tablespoons of the butter over medium heat. Add the rice and cook, stirring constantly, until light golden brown. Place in a 2-quart baking dish. Add the remaining tablespoon of butter to the same pan and cook the onion and mushrooms until the onions are golden. Add this to the baking dish, along with the beef broth, water, salt and pepper. Cover the dish and bake for 30 minutes, then remove the cover and bake for 10 minutes more until browned. Makes about 4 servings.

Mom's Macaroni Pie

This is good any time of the year as a change-of-pace side dish instead of rice or potatoes. When I was a child and Mom was making batches of this to freeze, I used to love to taste spoonfuls of the cooked macaroni and the rich, eggy, creamy sauce to help her decide if it had enough salt and pepper.

It was while watching Mom make Macaroni Pie that I learned two tricks that I still use today: 1) use white pepper instead of black pepper in light-colored sauces or dishes, when you don't want dark little flecks of pepper to show; and 2) if you dissolve the dry mustard in a tiny bit of water, it helps distribute it more evenly in another liquid, such as a sauce, and keeps you from ending up with hidden lumps of mustard that can taste bitter.

8 ounces small elbow macaroni
Salt, to taste
¾ stick butter
2 large eggs, lightly beaten
¾ cup evaporated milk
¾ cup water
White pepper, to taste
1 scant teaspoon dry mustard powder dissolved in just enough water to make a thin paste
8 ounces grated extra-sharp cheddar cheese

Preheat the oven to 375 degrees. Cook the macaroni in boiling, salted water until "al dente" (just slightly firm to the bite). Drain. Combine macaroni with all the remaining ingredients except the cheese; stir well. Taste and check for seasonings. Stir about one-quarter of the cheese into the macaroni mixture, then pour it into an 8-inch square baking dish. Sprinkle the rest of the cheese on top. Bake for 45 minutes-1 hour, until cheese is melted and bubbly. Makes 3-4 side-dish servings. Macaroni Pie freezes well. After pouring the macaroni mixture into the baking dish, cover it tightly and freeze. Sprinkle additional grated cheese on top right before baking. You don't have to thaw the pie first, but it will take a little longer to cook straight from the freezer.

Thanksgiving Sweet Potatoes

3 cups cooked, mashed sweet potatoes
1 cup sugar
2 large eggs
1 teaspoon vanilla extract
1 stick butter, melted
1 cup (packed) brown sugar
⅓ cup self-rising flour
1 cup chopped pecan pieces
⅓ cup butter, softened but not melted

This casserole is so rich that it's almost like dessert. We usually have it on Thanksgiving, which we spend at Edie's house. The streusel-style topping makes this a real winner.

Preheat the oven to 350 degrees. Mix the sweet potatoes, sugar, eggs, vanilla and melted butter together in a bowl. Pour the mixture into a buttered 13x9-inch casserole dish. In a small bowl, mix together the brown sugar, flour, pecans pieces and softened butter, using a fork to get the mixture to a crumbly consistency. Sprinkle this over the top of the casserole. Bake for 30 minutes, until the top is nicely browned. Makes 6-8 servings.

You can make the casserole a day before serving it. Simply spread the sweet potato mixture in the baking dish and refrigerate it. Stir together the nut mixture and sprinkle it on top right before you bake the dish.

King Street Shrimp Pie

N*o one in the family can remember how long we've been making this dish – but when shrimp-baiting season begins in September, we don't have any trouble remembering that this is one of our favorite shrimp recipes.*

8 slices day-old white bread, crusts removed
2 cups whole milk
2 large eggs, slightly beaten
4 tablespoons butter, melted
1 teaspoon salt
2-3 dashes Tabasco
Freshly-ground black pepper, to taste
1 rounded teaspoon dry mustard, dissolved in a little water
1 quart shrimp, cooked and peeled
Paprika

Preheat oven to 350 degrees. Tear the bread into roughly-shaped pieces and place them in a mixing bowl. Pour the milk over the bread and stir to coat. Stir in the eggs, melted butter, salt, Tabasco, pepper and mustard. Stir in the shrimp. Pour the mixture into a 1½-quart glass baking dish and top with a sprinkling of paprika. Bake 45 minutes-1 hour, until the top browns and the casserole has risen uniformly. Serve right away. Makes 4 servings.

Shrimp and Artichoke Casserole

For the sauce:

3½ tablespoons butter
4½ tablespoons all-purpose flour
¾ cup milk
¾ cup heavy whipping cream
Salt and white pepper, to taste
¼ cup dry sherry
1 tablespoon Worcestershire sauce

For the casserole:

3 tablespoons butter
8-ounce package fresh mushrooms, sliced
14-ounce can artichoke hearts, cut in quarters
1 pound raw shrimp, peeled and deveined
½ cup freshly-grated Parmesan cheese

We like serving this over rice, but you could use pasta just as well. The artichokes and Parmesan are terrific complements to the subtle sweetness of the shrimp.

Preheat the oven to 375 degrees. Lightly butter a 13x9-inch baking dish. To make the sauce: in a small saucepan over low heat (or in the top of a double-boiler set over simmering water), melt the 3½ tablespoons butter and the flour together, stirring constantly, until they form a smooth paste that's free of lumps. When the paste barely begins to bubble, add the milk and cream gradually, continuing to stir. Cook over medium-low heat until the sauce thickens, then season to taste with salt and white pepper. Remove the pan from the heat, stir in the sherry and the Worcestershire sauce, then set aside. To assemble the casserole: melt the 3 tablespoons butter in a skillet over medium heat. Add the mushroom slices and cook for 4-5 minutes, until they're softened and have released some of their liquid. To the prepared baking dish, add the artichoke hearts and the shrimp, followed by the cooked mushrooms. Pour the sauce over the top, then sprinkle with the Parmesan. Bake for 20-30 minutes, until the casserole is bubbly and golden on top. Serve at once over hot cooked rice. Makes about 4 servings.

Pasta and Shrimp with Blue Cheese Sauce

1⅓ pounds peeled raw shrimp
Juice of 1 lemon or lime
6 tablespoons butter
4 ounces cream cheese, softened
1⅓ ounces blue cheese
Cooked rice or pasta (for four)

South Carolina blue cheese, which is produced by hand in Clemson, is my first choice for this dish. After falling victim to distribution problems some years ago, Clemson blue cheese has become more widely available around the state in the past three or four years. Since Dad is a graduate of Clemson (class of 1942) and he loves blue cheese, I always think about him when I buy it, and when I make this rich dish.

Preheat the oven to 400 degrees. Spray a 9x13x2-inch casserole dish with nonstick cooking spray. Place the shrimp in the casserole dish and sprinkle the lemon or lime juice on top. In a saucepan over medium heat, melt the butter, cream cheese and blue cheese, stirring until combined. Pour the mixture over the shrimp. Bake for 20 minutes, until hot and bubbly Serve the shrimp and sauce over rice or pasta. Makes 4 servings.

Shrimp Pilau/Perlo/Pilaf

4 slices bacon
2 tablespoons butter, plus more if desired
¾ cup finely-chopped celery
Half of a medium green bell pepper, finely diced
1 pound raw shrimp, shelled and deveined
2 tablespoons Worcestershire sauce
2 tablespoons all-purpose flour (plus a little extra, if needed)
3 cups hot cooked rice

The preferred spelling for this shrimp-and-rice staple is somewhat up in the air. I grew up spelling it "pilau," but it's also spelled "pilaf" and is pronounced the way "perlo" looks. However you spell it, it's delicious.

An old family friend passed along the recipe many years ago; the source beyond that point isn't known to us.

In a large skillet, fry the bacon slices until crisp, then set aside to drain on paper towels. Crumble the bacon when it cools. Drain all but 2 tablespoons of bacon fat from the pan; to the remaining fat, add 2 tablespoons butter. Add the celery and bell pepper and cook until just tender. Spread the shrimp out on a plate and sprinkle the Worcestershire sauce over them, using your fingers to toss them slightly so all are coated with the sauce. Sprinkle the flour on top and toss the shrimp again so they're coated with flour. Add the shrimp to the skillet with the celery and bell pepper and cook until the shrimp are just done, no more than a couple of minutes. Add more flour to the skillet if needed so the shrimp don't stick. Add the cooked rice and stir gently to mix all the ingredients; if you wish, add some butter, to taste, so the rice is nice and moist. Serve the pilau hot, with the crumbled bacon on top. Makes about 6 servings.

Quail in White Wine Sauce

There have always been lots of hunters, male and female, in my family. This recipe, which appeared in the Charleston Junior League's **Charleston Receipts Repeats** *and originally called for doves and red wine, is one that Mom adapted for quail. Her version uses white wine and the lighter-colored Worcestershire sauce that's now available for use with poultry.*

4 tablespoons butter
1 medium onion, chopped
10-12 quail
Salt and freshly-ground black pepper, to taste
2 teaspoons dried parsley flakes
2 teaspoons light-colored Worcestershire sauce
¼ teaspoon dried thyme leaves
½ cup white wine, such as Sauvignon Blanc
1 cup chicken bouillon
Shake and Blend flour for gravy

In a large skillet over medium heat, melt the butter, then add the onions and sauté them until they're golden. Sprinkle the quail with salt and pepper, then add them to the pan, browning them on both sides. Add the parsley flakes, Worcestershire and thyme. Reduce the heat to a simmer. Arrange the quail so that the breast sides are up. Add the wine and bouillon, then reduce the heat to low. Cover the pan and cook 1 to 1½ hours, or until the quail are tender and cooked through. Push the quail to the edges of the pan and sprinkle a little of the Shake and Blend flour into the sauce, stirring to thicken it. When the sauce is the consistency you like, remove the quail from the pan and arrange on serving plates, spooning the sauce over the top. Makes 4 to 6 servings.

Good and Easy Venison

6-pound venison haunch or hindquarter, or loin roast
6-8 slices bacon
2 envelopes dry onion soup mix
2-3 bay leaves

Venison is notoriously dry, but this recipe avoids that problem. We like this roast on the Thanksgiving dinner table, right next to the turkey.

Preheat the oven to 350 degrees. Place the venison in a roasting pan (preferably one with a cover). Criss-cross the slices of bacon on top of the meat. Sprinkle the dry soup mix over the meat, then pour 1-2 cups of water in the bottom of the roasting pan. Add the bay leaves. Cover (use foil if your pan doesn't have a lid) and bake 3-4 hours, basting occasionally and watching for the meat to brown and become tender. A carving fork inserted into the thickest part should reveal the tenderness of beef. If desired, use pan drippings to make a gravy. Makes 6-8 servings.

Mom says you can use venison straight from the freezer for this recipe – no thawing needed.

Curried Chicken Divan

There are scads of chicken divan recipes out there, and heaven knows who came up with the first one. I've seen lots of versions, but what I like about this one is the use of curry powder. It adds a wonderful fragrance and an exotic kind of taste that sets the dish apart. It also makes this a particularly warming dish on a chilly night.

2 (10-ounce) packages frozen broccoli spears, thawed
3 boneless chicken breasts, about 4 ounces each, cut into bite-size chunks
2 (10-ounce) cans cream of chicken soup
1 cup mayonnaise
½ to ¾ teaspoon curry powder
1 teaspoon fresh lemon juice
½ cup grated sharp cheddar cheese
½ cup dry bread crumbs
1 tablespoon butter, melted

Preheat the oven to 350 degrees. Butter a 13x9x2-inch baking dish, then arrange the broccoli spears in the dish. Place the cubed chicken evenly around the dish on top of the broccoli. In a small bowl, mix together the soup, mayonnaise, curry powder and lemon juice. Pour this over the chicken and broccoli. Combine the cheese, bread crumbs and melted butter in a small bowl; mix lightly. Spread over the top of the casserole. Bake for 25-30 minutes, or until the sauce is hot and bubbly and the chicken and broccoli are cooked through. Makes 3-4 servings.

We used to make this using whole boneless chicken breasts, but I decided to make it easier on myself by cutting up the chicken a bit before cooking. As long as the chunks are good-sized, they don't cook too fast, and this is a good way to get some chicken in every spoonful.

Hot Crunchy Chicken Salad

1 tablespoon olive oil
5 tablespoons butter, divided
8-ounce package fresh cremini mushrooms, sliced
1 medium onion, diced
1 clove garlic, minced
3 cups diced, cooked chicken
3-4 cups cooked white rice
1 cup diced celery
1 teaspoon fresh lemon juice
1 (10-ounce) can cream of mushroom soup
1 tablespoon Dijon mustard
¾ cup mayonnaise
Salt and freshly-ground black pepper, to taste
1 cup cornflakes
½ cup sliced almonds

Preheat the oven to 350 degrees. In a skillet, melt the olive oil and 1 tablespoon of the butter over medium heat. Add the mushrooms, onion and garlic; sauté until the onions are golden. Drain off any excess fat, then place the mushroom mixture in a large mixing bowl. Add the chicken, rice, celery, lemon juice, soup, mustard, mayonnaise, salt and pepper; stir to combine well. Spread the mixture into a 13x9-inch casserole dish. In a small saucepan, melt the remaining 4 tablespoons of butter. Add the cornflakes and sliced almonds, stirring gently to coat. Sprinkle this mixture on top of the casserole. Bake for 30-35 minutes. If the topping starts getting too brown before the casserole is done, place a sheet of aluminum foil loosely on top and continue baking. Makes about 6 servings.

There's nothing particularly "fall-ish" about this family favorite's ingredients, but I do find myself keeping a casserole dish or two in the freezer during the fall. When the days seem to get busier and busier, it's great to be able to thaw the casserole during the day while we're at work, then just pop it in the oven at the end of a long day.

The recipe has made the rounds in a couple of different forms. I use fresh mushrooms, garlic and some Dijon mustard to give it an extra kick.

If you want to freeze the casserole, prepare it only to the point of spreading the mixture in the baking dish. Cover the dish tightly and freeze without the topping. When you're ready to bake, prepare the topping and add it just before you run the casserole in the oven.

Twisted Turkey

*E*verybody has leftover turkey after Thanksgiving dinner – often more than can be used in a safe amount of time. Refrigerated sliced turkey from the big dinner should be used within three or four days, according to current safe-food-handling guidelines.

After the obligatory turkey sandwiches on the Friday after Thanksgiving, we turn to this recipe to take care of the rest of the bird in a delicious way. This recipe came out of a magazine years ago; I think it originated with Pillsbury.

These bundles of flavor get their name from the way you twist together the points of the rolls that hold everything together.

3 ounces cream cheese, softened
3 tablespoons butter, melted, divided
2 cups cooked, cubed turkey
¼ teaspoon salt
¼ teaspoon freshly-ground black pepper
2 tablespoons milk
1 tablespoon chopped fresh chives
1 tablespoon chopped pimiento
1 (8-ounce) can crescent rolls
¼ cup (approximately) dry bread crumbs

Preheat the oven to 350 degrees. Blend the cream cheese and 2 tablespoons of the butter with a mixing spoon, until they're well combined. Add the turkey, salt, pepper, milk, chives and pimiento, stirring until well combined. Separate the crescent rolls into four rectangular sections, pressing the perforations together to seal. Spoon about ½ cup of the turkey mixture onto the center of each rectangle. Pull up the sides of the rolls, twisting the tops and pinching the side seams together to seal the turkey mixture inside. Place the bundles on a foil-lined baking sheet. When all the bundles are assembled, brush the top of each one with some of the remaining melted butter. Sprinkle the bread crumbs on top. Bake 20-25 minutes, until golden. Makes 3-4 light lunch servings, or 2-3 dinner servings.

...ken Tetrazzini

1 (4- to 5-pound) whole stewing chicken
3 (10-ounce) cans chicken broth
1 pound fresh mushrooms, sliced
1 green bell pepper, chopped
1 clove garlic, minced
4 tablespoons butter
3 tablespoons all-purpose flour
1¾ cups half-and-half (or more, if desired)
2 small bay leaves
8-10 ounces uncooked vermicelli or linguini pasta
¼ cup dry white wine
Salt and freshly-ground black pepper, to taste
2 large egg yolks, slightly beaten
Freshly-grated Parmesan cheese

Preheat the oven to 350 degrees. Butter a 2-quart casserole dish. Combine the chicken and broth in a large pot. Add water to cover the chicken if the broth doesn't do it. Cook over medium heat until the meat is tender. Remove the chicken, saving the broth; remove the skin and bones from the chicken and chop the meat. Strain the broth and reserve. In a large skillet, sauté the mushrooms, green pepper and garlic in the butter until the mushrooms and pepper are tender. Stir in the flour until it's well mixed. Stir in 1½ to 2 cups of the reserved broth, then gradually stir in the half-and-half. Stirring constantly, cook over low heat for 5 minutes, or until the mixture thickens. Meanwhile, in a large pot of boiling, salted water with the bay leaves added, begin cooking the pasta according to the directions on the package. To the sauce in the skillet, add the wine, salt and pepper and mix well. Add a small amount of the sauce to the beaten eggs yolks, stirring

Chicken isn't the only bird you can use in this dish; turkey works very well, and if you've got leftovers after Thanksgiving, this is a great way to polish them off quickly. Use 4-5 cups of chopped cooked turkey, and either turkey stock or chicken stock for the liquid in the sauce (to replace the liquid the chicken would have cooked in).

This is Edie's tried-and-true recipe.

to warm them. Then, add the egg yolk mixture to the sauce, stirring to combine. Add the chopped chicken. When the pasta is al dente, remove and discard the bay leaves. Drain the pasta and place it in the prepared casserole dish. Spoon the chicken and sauce on top and sprinkle generously with the Parmesan. Bake the casserole for 25-30 minutes, or until it's heated through. Makes 6 servings.

Apple Fritters

1 cup all-purpose flour
2 tablespoons sugar
1½ teaspoons baking powder
½ teaspoon salt
½ cup whole milk
1 large egg, beaten well
1 cup peeled chopped apple
Vegetable oil, for frying
Powdered sugar, for sprinkling on fritters

Sift together the flour, sugar, baking powder and salt. Stir in the milk; stir in the egg and mix well. Stir the apples into the batter. Drop the batter by large spoonfuls, two or three at a time, into deep, hot fat, and cook until the fritters are golden brown. Drain them on paper towels. Serve while hot, sprinkled with powdered sugar. Makes approximately 6 servings, depending on the size of the fritters.

South Carolina doesn't get as much apple attention as states such as Washington or even our sister, North Carolina. But towns such as Walhalla and Seneca in the northwestern corner of the Palmetto State raise some very fine apples every year, with varieties such as Granny Smith and Eastern Red Delicious among the most popular.

A small countertop fryer is great for making these fritters. Use a tart apple — one of those Granny Smiths, perhaps. They're so good, I'll bet you can't eat just one.

Elizabeth's Peanut Butter Candy

When I was about a month away from finishing work on this cookbook, my oldest sister, Elizabeth, passed away unexpectedly at the age of 46. Liz was always a good cook – she used to stand on a kitchen chair when she was little so she could watch Mom preparing different things.

I remember a high-school-age Liz making wonderful peanut butter fudge. I was too young then to realize that fudge can be tricky, but judging by Liz's results, I never would have concluded that. Hers always turned out delicious.

I usually use smooth peanut butter in this recipe, but crunchy works well, too.

1 cup (packed) light brown sugar
1 cup granulated sugar
⅓ cup light corn syrup
½ cup milk
1 tablespoon butter
5 tablespoons peanut butter
1 teaspoon vanilla extract

Butter an 8-inch square pan, then set it aside. In a heavy saucepan, combine the sugars, corn syrup and milk. Heat over medium heat, stirring constantly, until the mixture comes to a boil. Attach a candy thermometer to the saucepan and cook, without stirring, until the temperature reaches 234 degrees (soft ball stage). Keep a pastry brush and a bowl of water handy and, every so often, wet the brush and wipe down the sides of the saucepan to keep them free of sugar crystals. When the mixture reaches 234 degrees, remove the pan from the heat and add the butter and peanut butter. Let the saucepan stand undisturbed until the mixture cools to 110 degrees. At that time, remove the candy thermometer, add the vanilla, and begin beating the mixture rapidly with a wooden spoon. When it begins to lose its gloss, pour the mixture into the prepared pan. Using the tip of a very sharp, thin knife, mark the candy into the size squares you want. Let the candy cool completely, then cut into squares. Store the fudge in an airtight container. Makes about 2 dozen small squares.

Martha Washington

1 stick butter, softened
1 (16-ounce) box powdered sugar
4 tablespoons whipping cream
1 teaspoon vanilla extract
Extra powdered sugar (for coating the candy)
4 ounces milk chocolate
4 ounces bittersweet chocolate
4 tablespoons butter
2 (1-inch) squares paraffin
½ teaspoon vanilla

 he name of these sweet little bonbons is a mystery to me, but the source of their richness is no puzzle at all: butter, cream and powdered sugar — all covered with chocolate.

My sister Elizabeth loved making candies, and Martha Washington was one of her favorites. Box these up for gift-giving or take a pretty plate-full to a holiday drop-in, and people will think you're a master pastry chef. We just won't tell anyone how easy they are to make.

Cream butter until it's soft. Add powdered sugar gradually, beating until well combined (it will seem like there's way too much powdered sugar for the butter to absorb, but that's OK). Add the cream and vanilla and beat until the mixture comes together smoothly, stopping the mixer and using your hands if needed. Place some of the extra powdered sugar on a plate and rub a little on your hands. Roll the creamed mixture into smooth 1-inch balls, then in the powdered sugar. Place the balls on a wax-paper-lined cookie sheet. Place the candy in the refrigerator until firm, about 30-45 minutes. For coating, combine next 5 ingredients over low heat. Stir as the mixture melts and becomes smooth. Coat the balls of candy, one at a time, in the chocolate; use a fork to lift each one out of the chocolate and place it back on the waxed paper. When all the candies are coated, return the cookie sheet to the refrigerator for the chocolate to set, about 45 minutes. Makes about 40-50 candies. Store any leftovers in an airtight container in the refrigerator.

Brown Sugar Surprises

These moist, chewy bar cookies are a year-round favorite, but they're especially good in the fall when it's pecan time. We've been making these for as long as I can remember. Pack them in an airtight container and take them with you when you're tailgating before a football game.

1 cup (packed) light brown sugar
4 tablespoons butter, melted
1 large egg, lightly beaten
1 cup all-purpose flour
¾ cup chopped pecans
1 teaspoon baking powder
Pinch of salt
1 teaspoon vanilla extract

Preheat oven to 325 degrees. Lightly butter an 8x8-inch baking pan. Place the brown sugar in a mixing bowl. Add the melted butter and the egg; beat with an electric mixer until combined. Sprinkle a tablespoon or so of the flour over the nuts; stir to coat the nuts. Add the rest of the flour, the baking powder and salt to the brown sugar mixture; beat to combine (the mixture will be thick). Stir in the vanilla and the floured nuts. Spread the batter in the prepared pan and bake for 20-23 minutes, until light golden brown on top. Remove the pan to a wire rack to cool completely. (Squares will puff when baking, then fall slightly as they cool.) Makes 16-20 squares.

Banana Split Dessert

3 sticks butter, softened, divided
2 cups graham cracker crumbs
2 large eggs
2 cups powdered sugar
4 to 5 medium-size bananas
1 (20-ounce) can crushed pineapple, drained
1 (16-ounce) container prepared whipped topping
1 cup chopped pecans
Maraschino cherries, to garnish

Melt one of the sticks of butter. Place the graham cracker crumbs in a bowl, pour in the melted butter, and stir to combine. Press this mixture into the bottom of a 13x9x2-inch glass casserole. With an electric mixer, mix the eggs, the remaining sticks of butter, and the powdered sugar; beat until the mixture is extremely light and fluffy (10-15 minutes is ideal; use a standing mixer if you have one). Spread this mixture evenly over the crumb crust. Arrange the sliced bananas on top of the powdered sugar mixture. Spoon the crushed pineapple on top of the bananas. Cover with whipped topping. Sprinkle the chopped nuts evenly over the whipped topping, then arrange some cherries on top to complete the banana split effect. Refrigerate overnight before serving. Makes 12-15 servings.

When I was a student at Davidson College, many of us were members of small "houses" arranged in a horseshoe called Patterson Court. Houses offered meal plans that differed from the food in the cafeteria, and social activities as well. The setting was truly more home-like than a dorm. Each house had couches and easy chairs, big kitchens and dining rooms, and plenty of space to relax and talk or study.

I was a member of Rusk House (named for former Secretary of State Dean Rusk, who had taught at Davidson), and this Banana Split Cake was a favorite dessert of many "Ruskies." It's a good crowd cake because it's rich, and a little piece goes a long way. It should be made a day before serving so flavors can blend.

About the only thing a banana split has that this cake doesn't have is ice cream. Then again, the cake won't melt, so I guess it all balances out.

Cinnamon Ice Cream

*T*his is truly wonderful ice cream, and I have a former neighbor, chef Scott Roark, to thank for it. For years, Scott was the chef/owner of a Mount Pleasant restaurant called the Village Cafe, and he served as the culinary arts program coordinator at Trident Technical College in Charleston before a recent move to the Upstate.

Scott gave me this recipe several years ago for a story I was writing about cinnamon, and now it's become a frequent part of our Thanksgiving dinner.

Put a scoop of this alongside a piece of apple pie and you'll be in heaven.

1 quart half-and-half
1 vanilla bean, split lengthwise
2 cinnamon sticks
10 egg yolks
10 ounces sugar
2 teaspoons ground cinnamon

In a saucepan, heat the half-and-half with the vanilla bean and cinnamon sticks to scalding, then take the saucepan off the heat. Remove the vanilla bean and, using the back of a paring knife, scrape the seeds back into the half-and-half. Let the half-and-half steep off the heat for 30 minutes, leaving the cinnamon sticks in. In a mixing bowl, beat the egg yolks, sugar and ground cinnamon until light and fluffy. Slowly pour the half-and-half into the whipped egg yolk mixture while whisking rapidly. Place the bowl over simmering water, stirring constantly with a whisk or wooden spoon, until it thickens enough to coat the spoon. Take care not to overheat, which will coagulate the custard. Remove the bowl from the heat and continue to stir the custard for a few seconds to keep it from overcooking where it touches the hot bowl. Let the mixture cool slightly, then cover and refrigerate it overnight. To make the ice cream, remove the custard from the refrigerator, take out the cinnamon sticks and then process the custard in an ice cream maker, following the manufacturer's instructions. Transfer the ice cream to a chilled container and store, covered, in the freezer. Makes about 2 quarts.

Holiday Ice Cream

½ gallon vanilla ice cream
12-18 macaroons
1 (10-ounce) jar maraschino cherries, drained
½ cup sherry

Remove the ice cream from the freezer and place it in a large mixing bowl to soften (save the container). Break the macaroons into bite-size chunks and cut the cherries into quarters. When the ice cream is softened, add the macaroons, cherries and sherry, stirring quickly to combine. Return the ice cream to its container and return it to the freezer immediately to harden. Allow several hours before serving. Makes ½ gallon.

Although this ice cream is good any time, it somehow seems especially delicious served in a pretty sherbet dish at the end of a nice holiday dinner.

You'll need macaroons for this recipe – either purchased or homemade. We like the recipe inside the label of the 8-ounce cans of Solo Pure Almond Paste. It makes twice as many macaroons as you'll need for the ice cream – but the extras freeze well in a zipper-top plastic bag for future use in this or other dishes.

You can easily adjust the amounts of cherries and macaroons to suit your family's tastes. Don't tinker with the amount of sherry here, because using too much will prevent the ice cream from hardening properly.

Winter

Winter

*M*ost of all I remember those cold afternoons when the sun was sliding down behind the trees and the evening chill began to descend on my small home town.

Usually, I was riding home on my bicycle, late for supper, flying through the neighborhoods, head down low on the handlebars to resist the wind, knowing that the warmth of my mother's kitchen would warm my body and soul as soon as I rushed in the back door.

These were the days when sundown came sooner than expected and winter made itself known to us. This cold spell was the small price we paid for a lifetime of languid, sultry summers spent sweating and cursing the heat.

Winter always came upon us like a shade being drawn down across our eyes, one of God's subtle reminders of who is charge. And while we knew the afternoons eventually would lengthen again to their original splendor, we always felt as if they might not.

That is why we huddled together in front of fireplaces, fighting off winter's wrath the only way Southerners know how, sipping soups and buttering cornbread, as we waited impatiently for spring.

The smells of my childhood still conjure up images I cannot deny.

On cold, late afternoons I vividly recall the

smell of wood smoke from the colored section of town as it rode the wind through our neighborhoods, leaving behind the unmistakable odors of fatback and collards.

These were days when Betty Crocker and Aunt Jemima were household names, but, in reality, lived in different households. Yet black or white, Southern women have an inherent gift that transforms them into angels in anybody's kitchen. They are the secret ingredient that makes biscuits rise and corn cakes crackle and pot roast piping hot with perfection.

But there is no stereotypical mother in my mind. They are all our mothers rolled into one. They are the ones who wore the aprons of love around their waists and popped your hand with a spatula if you tried to sneak a bit of fried chicken before dinner. And they were the ones who stood there in business suits, high heel shoes and makeup, magically producing chicken pot pies after a long day at the office.

Either way, it was their gentle hand, their loving touch, their beautiful gift of sustenance that made little boys on bicycles pedal faster as they hurried home for supper on those cold, wintry afternoons so long ago.

Praline Coffee Cake

5 tablespoons cold butter, cut in chunks
1 cup packed light brown sugar
2 teaspoons cinnamon
¾ cup coarsely-chopped pecans
1 stick butter, softened
¾ cup sugar
1 teaspoon vanilla extract
3 large eggs
2 cups all-purpose flour
1 teaspoon baking powder
1 teaspoon baking soda
1 teaspoon salt
1 cup sour cream

*Any recipe with "praline" in the title immediately gets my attention. This coffee cake is a delicious take on that creamy, pecan-studded candy. The recipe is from the no-longer-in-print **Post-Courier Cookbook**, a collection of Loved & Lost columns by the paper's first food editor, Charlotte Walker. The cookbook was published in 1966.*

Preheat the oven to 350 degrees. Grease and flour a 10-inch tube pan. Place the butter in a small bowl, and add the brown sugar and cinnamon. Using a pastry blender or two knives, cut in the butter until the mixture is crumbly. Add the pecans and stir. Set aside. In a mixing bowl, beat the softened butter, sugar and vanilla until fluffy. Beat in the eggs, one at a time. Sift together the flour, baking powder, baking soda and salt. Add these dry ingredients to the butter mixture alternately with the sour cream, beginning and ending with the dry ingredients. Spread a little more than half the batter in the bottom of the prepared pan, then sprinkle half of the brown sugar-nut mixture over the top. Add the rest of the batter, then sprinkle the remaining nut mixture on the top. Bake for 40-50 minutes, or until a toothpick inserted in cake comes out clean. Cool the cake in the pan on a wire rack for 10 minutes, then turn it out onto the rack. Serve warm or at room temperature. Makes 12-14 servings.

This coffee cake can be a little crumbly if you slice it while it's too hot. Let it cool down to warm, then slice it using a serrated knife.

White Hot Chocolate

Yes, I know. White chocolate isn't real chocolate because it doesn't contain the dark "liquor" that makes chocolate what it is. That doesn't make a bit of difference to a fan like me. I think it's almost as good as "chocolate" chocolate and I'd hate to think of any time of year, especially the holidays, without them both.

This very rich twist on basic hot chocolate should warm body and soul on a cold day. It's another recipe that I clipped from the paper years ago, without keeping track of the source.

3½ cups milk
2 tablespoons sugar
3½ ounces white chocolate, finely chopped
1 ounce milk chocolate, finely chopped
Crème de cacao (optional)

In a heavy saucepan, heat the milk and sugar to just below a boil. Remove the pan from the heat and add both kinds of chocolate. Let stand for 2 minutes. Transfer the mixture to a blender and whip it until it's frothy. Add the crème de cacao, if desired. Serve hot. Makes 6 servings, about 1 cup each.

When buying white chocolate, look for cocoa butter in the ingredient list. It makes the richest, fullest-tasting white chocolate. Products that contain partially hydrogenated oils are frequently of less desirable quality. Some of the top quality white chocolate brands you might see in your grocery store are made by Lindt and Ghirardelli.

Sweet Potato Muffins with Ginger Butter

¾ cup packed light brown sugar
1¾ cups all-purpose flour
2 teaspoons baking powder
¼ teaspoon baking soda
¼ teaspoon salt
¾ teaspoon ground cinnamon
¼ teaspoon ground ginger
¾ cup mashed, baked sweet potato (cooled)
2 large eggs, at room temperature, lightly beaten
½ cup milk, at room temperature
3 tablespoons vegetable oil
1½ teaspoons vanilla extract
⅓ cup finely-chopped crystallized ginger — *did not use just added extra ginger s sugar/cin on top.*

*C*rystallized ginger gives these muffins — and the accompanying flavored butter — their distinctive spicy taste. I came across the recipe while doing a feature story on ginger several years ago.

Preheat the oven to 375 degrees. Lightly spray 12 standard muffin cups with nonstick cooking spray. In a large mixing bowl, whisk together the brown sugar, flour, baking powder, baking soda, salt, cinnamon and ground ginger. In another bowl, combine the sweet potato, eggs, milk, oil and vanilla; stir together until well-mixed. Hollow out a well in the center of the flour mixture, then add the sweet potato mixture, stirring just until the dry ingredients are moistened. Stir in the crystallized ginger. Spoon the batter into the prepared muffin cups, filling each one about two-thirds full. Bake for 15-20 minutes, or until a toothpick inserted in the center comes out clean. Place the muffin tin on a wire rack and let the muffins cool for 5 minutes, then turn them out of the pan. Serve while warm with

Ginger Butter. Store any leftovers in an airtight container at room temperature. Makes 12 muffins.

Ginger Butter

1 stick butter, at room temperature
1 tablespoon honey
2 tablespoons finely-chopped crystallized ginger

In a bowl, stir together all the ingredients until they're well combined. Serve immediately with warm Sweet Potato Ginger Muffins, or place the butter in small crock or mold and refrigerate it until ready to serve. If refrigerated, the butter should stand at room temperature for about 15 minutes before you serve it.

Coffee Punch

4 cups strong coffee, sweetened to taste
⅔ pint milk
½ pint whipping cream
Vanilla extract, to taste
1 quart vanilla ice cream

Thoroughly chill the coffee, milk, whipping cream and vanilla, then combine all four in a punch bowl. Soften the ice cream slightly, then add it in several portions to the punch, stirring gently. Makes 20 punch-cup-size servings.

Punch is still in style at holiday parties around here, and this one is popular as can be. It tastes like extra-rich iced coffee. The recipe has had a long life in various family members' collections.

Hot Clemson Blue Cheese Dip

When I wrote a story about the blue cheese that's made in Clemson, S.C., back in December of 1999, I got on a blue cheese kick that lasted for weeks. This worked out well, since I'd bought several pounds of the cheese while I was in Clemson for the interviews.

I came across a recipe for this rich blue cheese dip in a wire-service story, and it sounded wonderful, so I took it over to Mom's for pre-Christmas-dinner munching that year. It was an unqualified success. I have since tinkered with it just a bit, and it's even more divine than before.

Use a chafing dish or small Crock-Pot to keep this warm.

12 ounces cream cheese, cut into cubes
6 ounces blue cheese, crumbled
½ cup half-and-half
4 slices bacon, cooked crisp and crumbled
3 cloves garlic, finely minced
2 tablespoons chopped fresh chives
5 tablespoons coarsely chopped smoked almonds

In a small saucepan, combine the cream cheese, blue cheese, half-and-half, cooked bacon and minced garlic. Place the pan over low heat, heating until the cheese melts; stir constantly. Stir in the chives. Place the cheese mixture in a chafing dish, fondue pot, or warmed small Crock-Pot. Sprinkle the chopped smoked almonds on top. Keep warm and serve with assorted crackers. Makes about 1¾ to 2 cups.

Spoonbread

1 cup cornmeal (yellow or white)
1 tablespoon butter, plus more for buttering the baking dish
1 teaspoon salt
1 cup boiling water
1 cup milk
1½ teaspoons baking powder
1 large egg, separated

Spoonbread is true, corn-y Southern comfort. I especially like it with some good sausage on a chilly night. Yellow cornmeal is my preference, but white works just as well.

Preheat the oven to 375 degrees. Place the cornmeal, butter and salt in a mixing bowl. Pour the boiling water on top, stir, then let the mixture stand until it's cool. Stir in the milk, baking powder and egg yolk. In a small bowl, beat the egg white until firm peaks form. Fold the egg white into the cornmeal mixture. Butter an 8-inch or 9-inch square casserole or baking dish and pour in the cornmeal mixture. Bake for 30-40 minutes, until the spoonbread is light golden brown on top. Serve immediately with butter. Makes 3-4 side-dish servings.

Red Cabbage Slaw with Blue Cheese, Pecans and Bacon

Here's another terrific recipe from Holly Herrick. Clemson blue cheese and pecans from the Piedmont area team up with cabbage to make this slaw hearty and satisfying..

1 medium head red cabbage, cored, quartered and thinly sliced
¼ cup balsamic vinegar
⅓ cup light olive oil
Salt and freshly-ground black pepper, to taste
7 slices bacon, cut into cubes, cooked and drained
½ cup chopped pecans
½ teaspoon sugar
4 scallions, cleaned and cut into a fine dice
⅓ cup blue cheese

The warm pecans and bacon add a nice temperature contrast to the slaw. If they cool off while you're assembling the salad, just pop them in a warm oven briefly and they'll heat right back up.

In a large bowl, toss the cabbage with the vinegar, oil, salt and pepper, to taste. Cover with plastic wrap and let it stand at room temperature for at least 3 hours, and up to 5 hours. Cook the bacon over medium-high heat until crispy and golden brown. Remove to paper towels to drain, and discard all but ½ teaspoon of the bacon fat. In the same pan, heat the fat again over low heat, then add the pecans; cook until they're golden, stirring often, about 3 minutes. Season with the sugar, salt and pepper while still hot; set on a paper towel to drain. To make the slaw, remove the cabbage from the refrigerator and toss; taste to verify seasoning. Arrange some cabbage in the center of eight serving plates. Sprinkle with some of the scallions, then top with a sprinkle of blue cheese, warm nuts and warm bacon. Finish with a touch of coarse black pepper. Serve immediately. Makes 8 servings.

Christmas Day Spinach Casserole

1 pound fresh spinach, washed and trimmed
4 tablespoons butter
¼ cup all-purpose flour
1 teaspoon salt
⅛ teaspoon cayenne pepper
1½ cups milk
1 cup fresh (not dry) bread crumbs
2 hard-boiled eggs, thinly sliced
1 cup shredded sharp cheddar cheese
1 strip bacon, cooked and crumbled

Preheat the oven to 350 degrees. Bring a large pot of salted water to a boil and cook the spinach, covered, until tender, about 5-7 minutes. Drain the spinach so it is as dry as possible, then chop coarsely. Use a paper towel to blot up any excess liquid. In a small pan, melt the butter over medium-low heat, then blend in the flour, salt and pepper to make a smooth, lump-free paste. Stir in the milk slowly and bring the heat up to medium-high, stirring constantly for about 3 minutes; the sauce will thicken and become bubbly. Remove the pan from the heat. Butter a 6-cup oblong casserole dish. Layer the ingredients as follows: half of the bread-crumbs; half of the spinach; half of the egg slices; one-third of the sauce; one-half of the cheddar; the rest of the spinach; the rest of the egg slices; another one-third of the sauce; the rest of the cheddar; the remaining third of the sauce; and the remaining crumbs. Sprinkle the bacon crumbles evenly over the top. Bake uncovered for 35-40 minutes. Makes 4 servings.

This very rich casserole is a fixture on the Christmas dinner table at Mom's house, right along with her roast beef tenderloin and the "Squash Boats" that the kids love.

This recipe appeared in a women's magazine years ago, and it was attributed to a former cook at Middleton Place, a plantation near Charleston.

Instead of fresh spinach, you can use 2 (10-ounce) packages of frozen chopped spinach. Cook and drain thoroughly, then let the spinach cool enough for you to be able to pick it up in your hands and squeeze out the excess water.

We think that this dish is prettiest when assembled right before cooking. If you put it together too far ahead of time, the spinach tends to give the cream sauce and egg whites a rather unappetizing green color!

Sally Lunn

1 stick butter
½ cup sugar
3 large eggs
1 cup milk
2 cups all-purpose flour
1 tablespoon baking powder
½ teaspoon salt

Sally Lunn is a mildly sweet Southern bread served warm with butter as a side dish. Think of it as a smoother-textured, lightly-sweetened cornbread. A bowl of soup with some Sally Lunn makes a nice cool-weather lunch or light supper.

This recipe has passed through the hands of several members of the family.

Preheat the oven to 350 degrees. Grease a tube pan. In a mixing bowl, cream the butter and sugar together until blended. In another bowl, beat the eggs, then beat in the milk. To the flour, add the baking powder and the salt. Add the flour mixture and the milk mixture alternately to the shortening mixture, beating after each addition (begin and end with some of the flour mixture). Pour the batter into the prepared pan and bake for 30-40 minutes, until golden brown. Serve at once, hot, with butter. Makes 10-12 servings.

Creamy Corn Off the Cob

5 or 6 good-size ears fresh corn
¼ cup milk, plus more if needed
⅛ cup whipping cream
5 tablespoons butter, softened
Salt and white pepper, to taste

Cut the kernels from the ears of corn and, using the edge of the knife, scrape down the sides of each ear to release the "milk." You should have about 4 cups kernels, more or less. Place the kernels and the milky liquid from the corn in a saucepan. Add the remaining ingredients. Place the saucepan over medium heat and heat slowly, stirring frequently, until the mixture is at a steady bubble. Reduce the heat and simmer for about 20 minutes, until the "sauce" that develops is creamy and slightly thickened (you might need to add a bit more milk). Taste and adjust seasonings if needed. Makes 4-6 servings.

It's hard for us not to stand at the stove and eat spoonfuls of this stuff right out of the pot – that's how delicious it is. Yes, it's rich and fattening, which is why we make it only for special occasions. Once you taste it, it's hard to resist the urge to make more and more and more ...

If your corn isn't nice and lightly sweet on its own, add just a pinch of sugar to the pot.

New Southern Cabbage

*T*his recipe was developed by Marion Sullivan, the wonderful cookbook columnist for *The Post and Courier.* Here's what she tells me about this dish: "Cooking cabbage in a 'New Southern' manner is different in two ways from the old-fashioned method in which cabbage is stewed until it is almost beige in color and soft enough to eat with a spoon. Here, cabbage is purchased that has some of its outer, dark green leaves, which provide color, and it is sautéed until just tender. You'll get more nutrition as well as a better-looking dish."

1 small (1½-pound) cabbage, cored, quartered and sliced ½-inch thick, with dark green slices kept separate from light slices
2 tablespoons unsalted butter
1 tablespoon minced garlic
½ cup chopped yellow onion
⅔ cup chicken stock
Salt and freshly-ground black pepper

Bring a large frying pan or skillet of water to a boil over medium-high heat. Drop in the slices of dark green cabbage and simmer for 4 minutes. Add the light slices and simmer until all are just tender, about 5 minutes more. Drain and rinse with cold water to stop the cooking process. Drain well. Heat the butter in the frying pan over medium heat. Add the garlic and onion, cover, and cook for 2 minutes. Add the chicken stock and cook, uncovered, until the stock has almost evaporated and looks like a glaze; stir frequently to prevent scorching. Add the cabbage and stir until it is heated through, about 4 minutes. Season with salt and pepper to taste and serve. Makes 6 servings.

Leslie's Hash Brown Casserole

1 stick plus 2 tablespoons butter, divided
¾ cup chopped onion
1 (32-ounce) bag frozen hash brown potatoes,
thawed enough to break apart when stirred
1 (10¾ ounce) can cream of chicken or cream of
mushroom soup
1 cup sour cream
10 ounces grated sharp cheddar cheese
Salt and freshly-ground black pepper, to taste
2 cups cornflakes

Preheat the oven to 350 degrees. In a skillet, melt 1 stick of the butter and sauté the onion until golden. Place the onions, hash browns, soup, sour cream, cheese, salt and pepper in a large mixing bowl and stir to combine well. Spread the mixture into a 13x9x2-inch baking dish. In a small saucepan, melt the remaining 2 tablespoons of butter over low heat, then add the corn flakes and stir gently to coat them with the butter. Distribute the cornflakes evenly over the top of the casserole. Bake the casserole for 1 hour, until it's hot and bubbly. Makes 6-8 servings.

I'm not sure where this popular recipe originated, but for us it came from family friend Leslie Shearin Painter. It's very easy and makes a real crowd-pleaser of a casserole.

The one thing I've changed is that, instead of dotting the cornflake topping with butter, I melt some butter and stir that together with the cornflakes. That way, every part of the crunchy topping is buttery good. However, this is indeed a fat-rich dish; if you prefer to cut back, you can sprinkle the plain cornflakes on top without adding any butter. This dish also works well with the reduced-fat versions of the soup, sour cream and cheese.

Donna's Pineapple au Gratin

I have to tell you, the first time this unusual side dish was described to me, I thought it sounded awful. If it sounds that way to you, too, keep an open mind and give it a taste. I did, and I'm a convert.

This is very rich, so a little goes a long way. We think it's nice with ham at the holidays. Donna Frazier, a family friend, shared the recipe with us a few years ago.

2 (approximately 20-ounce) cans pineapple tidbits, with juices
1 cup sugar
6 tablespoons all-purpose flour
2 cups grated sharp cheddar cheese
Ritz cracker crumbs
1 stick butter, melted

Preheat the oven to 350 degrees. Grease a 1½-quart casserole dish. In a bowl, stir together the pineapple tidbits and their juices, the sugar, flour and cheese. Pour the mixture into the prepared dish. Cover the top with cracker crumbs, then pour the melted butter evenly over the top. Bake for 25 minutes, or until bubbly and rich golden on top. Makes 6-8 servings.

Happy New Year Hoppin' John

I usually cook the peas (one 12-ounce package of red field peas, field peas or cowpeas) on New Year's Eve. These peas are used for their wonderful flavor in this recipe. They're widely available in supermarkets in the South, and usually have cooking directions on the package. Just in case your package does not have directions, I usually spread out the dry peas on a tray and remove any little rocks or foreign bodies from the peas. Rinse the peas in cold water, then put them in a large pot or Dutch oven and cover with 2 inches of water. Allow to soak overnight. Pour off this first water and add enough fresh water to cover peas by 2-3 inches. A ham hock cooked with the peas adds flavor. Add salt – 1 tablespoon or to your taste. Cook the peas over medium to low heat until they are tender. They will darken and turn a rich brown color. Stir them occasionally as they cook and add more water, if necessary. Refrigerate the peas in the cooking liquid overnight.

On New Year's Day, I warm them up and drain the peas (a collander is good for this) and save both the peas and the juice in which they have been cooked. Next, rinse 2 cups of rice, drain well and put in a rice steamer with 2 cups of the reserved cooking liquid from the peas. Fry 4 slices of bacon until crisp, and drain on paper towels. Set aside. In the same frying pan, lightly brown 1 medium onion (chopped or diced) in the bacon drippings. Add the onions and the drippings to the steamer of rice. If you are concerned about the amount of fat in the pan, you can let your conscience be your guide as to the amount you use. I'm inclined to

When Christmas is over, Lowcountry cooks begin to plan for a festive New Year. Most wouldn't consider skipping the Hoppin' John, as it ensures a happy new year. This dish is cherished by all – except, perhaps, the children, who need to eat at least a teaspoonful "for luck." For wealth in the year ahead, greens, particularly collards, are the order of the day. The rest of the meal is up to you and tradition, and if Mother or Grandmother always added macaroni pie and some ambrosia for dessert, then you have your own choices and traditions to establish. Hot Curried Fruit or Emma Law's Cranberry Sauce will add color and flavor.

Sometimes it just doesn't seem right to force a tried-and-true recipe – one that's always been made with a bit of this and a pinch of that – into the constrictions of a format. This is one of those times.

Hoppin' John, a rice-and-peas (beans) dish, is a Lowcountry New Year's tradition. When I asked my mother to try to write down exactly how she made it, it was no easy task; she's always made it by heart. She gave me this description and asked me to shape it up into the formula I needed. Sorry, Mom – I'm not touching it. It's great as is. Here are her instructions for Hoppin' John.

say that since New Year's comes but once a year, a little bacon drippings probably won't be too much of a problem. Steam the rice for about 30-45 minutes, then stir with a fork. Add 2 cups – or more, if you like – of the cooked and drained peas, stirring them into the rice with the fork. Taste for seasonings and add, if necessary, some salt, black pepper, or red (cayenne) pepper. Cook until the rice is done, about 30 minutes more. Serve with the crisp bacon crumbled on top.

Hoppin' John is wonderful with ham or roast pork, and delicious with game. It can be frozen (I use the double-thick freezer bags with enough in each bag for a single meal). This recipe makes about 10 cups of delicious Hoppin' John, enough to serve about 8 people.

Squash Boats

4 medium-size yellow squash
Salt, to taste
1 egg, beaten
⅛ cup bread crumbs or cracker crumbs
1 tablespoon butter, melted
1 teaspoon hot English mustard paste
Red pepper and/or freshly-ground black pepper
Finely-grated sharp or extra-sharp cheddar cheese, to taste

My nephew and niece, Andrew and Mary Magill Blair, christened these stuffed squash halves as "squash boats" several years ago, and the name has stuck. We make these a part of many dinners, especially Thanksgiving and Christmas, so the kids have their own special favorite dish on the table.

You can assemble these ahead of time and store them covered, in the refrigerator, until it's baking time.

Preheat the oven to 350 degrees. Boil the squash in salted water until just tender (leave the blossom and stem ends of the squash attached). Drain. When the squash are cool enough to handle, cut off the ends, and slice each squash in half lengthwise. Using a small spoon, scoop out the flesh in the center of each squash, leaving a hollowed-out space; place the scooped-out squash in a mixing bowl. To that, add the remainder of the ingredients, stirring to combine. Place the squash shells on a foil-lined baking sheet, cut sides up. Fill each hollowed-out area with the squash-egg mixture. Bake the squash for 15-20 minutes, until heated through. Makes 4 servings (2 "boats" per person).

Christmas Day Roast Beef Tenderloin

Roast beef is as much a part of our Christmas dinner as venison and turkey are at Thanksgiving. What we like about this simple, three-ingredient coating is that it enhances the flavor of the tenderloin, rather than covering it up. Heaven knows, when you pay what you pay for tenderloin, you sure want to be able to taste it! If you find yourself wanting a little more of the coating, though, this recipe is easy to double.

2 teaspoons Dijon mustard
2 teaspoons Coleman's dry mustard
2 teaspoons sugar
4 pounds (approximately) beef tenderloin
Salt, to taste

Preheat the oven to 425 degrees. Combine the mustards and the sugar in a small bowl, stirring to combine. Place the tenderloin in a roasting pan and make a few shallow cuts in the surface, then rub the mustard mixture into the meat. Let it stand at room temperature for 45 minutes. Sprinkle the meat with salt, place the pan in the oven, and cook the roast at 425 degrees for 45 minutes. Without removing the meat from the oven, cut the temperature down to 325 degrees and continue cooking for another 15 minutes per pound, or until the meat reaches the desired level of doneness.

To check how done the meat is, use an instant-read meat thermometer inserted in the thickest part of the toast. For beef that is medium-rare at the center, the temperature should be 140-145 degrees. The meat will continue to cook a little, and the temperature will rise a bit, even after the roast is out of the oven. Remove the tenderloin from the oven and let stand 10 minutes before carving. Makes 6-8 servings.

Lowcountry Veal Stew

3 pounds veal cubes
½ cup canola oil
½ cup all-purpose flour
1 tablespoon minced garlic
1 onion, chopped
¾ cup chopped green onion
¾ cup chopped celery
1 cup chopped green bell pepper
½ cup crushed tomato
2 teaspoons salt
Freshly-ground black pepper
½ teaspoon ground thyme
2 bay leaves
¾ cup water
¾ cup red wine
¼ teaspoon hot pepper sauce
1½ tablespoons Worcestershire sauce
5 tablespoons chopped fresh parsley

Veal has an unheralded place in Charleston's culinary history. Many farmers didn't want to give over a lot of valuable land for cattle to graze on, so veal, needed less space, gained a prominent place on Carolina tables.

This stew is great for a casual company supper because you can make it in the morning, refrigerate it during the day for the flavors to blend, then reheat it right before serving. It's another winning recipe from my sister Edie.

Brown the veal cubes in the oil in a large skillet. Remove the meat to a bowl. Stir the flour into the pan drippings and cook over low heat for several minutes, until dark brown, stirring constantly. Add the garlic, onion, green onion, celery and bell pepper; sauté until the vegetables are limp. Add the tomato, salt and pepper; simmer for 5 minutes, stirring constantly. Add the thyme, bay leaves, water, wine, pepper sauce and Worcestershire; mix well. Add the veal and simmer for 1 hour, stirring occasionally. Discard the bay leaves, then stir in the chopped parsley. Pour the stew into a bowl and refrigerate, covered, for several hours so the flavors can develop. Reheat the stew just before it's time to eat. Serve with rice or mashed potatoes. Makes 8 servings.

Savory Sausage Casserole

It's been said that pork is the defining flavor of Southern cooking, and pork sausage is what makes this casserole a meal in a dish. Other than the pork and rice, there's not too much Southern about this recipe. But it's a longtime family favorite that makes an easy and warming supper.

1 pound bulk pork sausage
1 cup uncooked rice
2 (2-ounce) envelopes chicken noodle soup mix
¼ cup finely-chopped onion
1 cup chopped celery
2 cups water
1 tablespoon soy sauce
½ cup toasted, slivered, blanched almonds

Preheat the oven to 350 degrees. Brown the sausage in a skillet over medium heat, using a fork to crumble it as it cooks. When the sausage is cooked through, remove the skillet from the heat and drain off the fat. In a bowl, stir together the sausage, rice, dry soup mix, onion and celery. Spread mixture into a 2-quart casserole dish. At this point, the casserole may be covered and refrigerated for several hours, if desired. When ready to cook, mix the water and soy sauce and pour it over the casserole. Add the almonds and stir gently to mix everything together. Cover the dish with aluminum foil and bake for 1 hour. Makes 4-6 servings.

Slow-Cooked Beef Stew

2 pounds lean stew meat, cut in cubes
⅔ cup all-purpose flour
Salt and freshly-ground black pepper
4 carrots, peeled and sliced into ¼-inch rings
4 large potatoes, peeled and chopped
1 onion, chopped
1 clove garlic, finely minced
1 cup beef stock
2 tablespoons Worcestershire sauce
2 teaspoons Kitchen Bouquet
2 bay leaves

Place the meat in the insert of a 4-quart (or larger) Crock-Pot. Sprinkle the flour on top, then add salt and pepper according to your preference. Stir the cubes of meat so they're coated with the flour. Add the remainder of the ingredients to the Crock-Pot and stir to combine everything. Cook on the low setting for 8-9 hours; the meat should be cooked through, the vegetables tender and the gravy thickened. Serve over hot cooked rice, or by itself. Makes 4-6 servings.

Crock-Pot slow cookers seem to have come back in fashion recently. No wonder. It's hard to beat the experience of opening the door after a long day at work and inhaling the fragrance of dinner – already prepared and waiting on you.

Ken and I like this old-fashioned stew over rice, but it's also good by itself, served up in a hearty bowl.

Lemon Pepper Eye of Round

Mom gave me this simple recipe years ago for one of the first "company's coming" suppers I'd ever attempted. It's just as good and easy now as it was back then.

To get the best and freshest meat possible, I take full advantage of having a wonderful butcher shop near my house. Although eye of round can sometimes be tough, I find that this version turns out consistently tender and juicy.

2½ pounds (approximately) eye of round roast
1 (16-ounce) bottle "zesty" Italian salad dressing
1 (8-ounce) bottle soy sauce
Meat tenderizer
Vegetable oil
Lemon pepper seasoning

Use a large fork to poke holes several times in the meat. Place the meat in a heavy, zipper-top plastic bag, then pour in the dressing and soy sauce (you can use less of these two ingredients for a smaller piece of meat, but keep the proportions more or less the same). Refrigerate the meat for at least 12 hours, preferably 24 hours. When you're ready to cook, preheat the oven to 350 degrees. Remove the meat from the bag and discard the marinade. Sprinkle the meat on all sides with meat tenderizer. Add a thin layer of vegetable oil to a large skillet – just enough oil to coat the bottom of the pan. Heat the pan until the oil is very hot, then add the meat, searing it. Turn the meat so that all sides sear to a nice rich brown. Place the meat in a roasting pan, then rub lemon pepper seasoning generously onto all surfaces of the meat. Roast the meat, uncovered, until it reaches the desired doneness according to an instant-read meat thermometer inserted into the thickest part of the roast. For medium-rare, the temperature should be 145 degrees. A 2½-pound roast should take 60-75 minutes. Makes 5-6 servings.

Parade Day Chewy Ginger Cookies

1½ sticks butter, softened
1 cup sugar
1 teaspoon baking powder
1 teaspoon baking soda
1½ to 2 teaspoons ground ginger to taste
½ teaspoon ground cinnamon
¼ teaspoon ground cloves
¼ teaspoon salt
1 large egg
⅓ cup molasses
2⅔ cups all-purpose flour
1 cup turbinado sugar (Sugar in the Raw)
½ cup very finely-chopped crystallized ginger

Ken and I sometimes invite a few folks to our house before the annual Holiday Parade in Mount Pleasant. We make a few big batches of hot chocolate and serve these chewy cookies, then everybody walks over to the watch the parade pass by. (We live just a short way from the route.)

The turbinado sugar that coats these cookies makes them sparkle on the plate – literally. Those tiny golden-colored cubes seem to catch the light in such a pretty way.

*This is my tinkered-with version of a recipe that I first saw in **Cookies for Christmas** (Meredith).*

Preheat the oven to 375 degrees. In a large mixing bowl, using an electric mixer, cream the butter on medium speed until smooth and fluffy. Add the sugar, baking powder, baking soda, ginger, cinnamon, cloves and salt. Beat on medium to medium-high until well combined, scraping down the sides of the bowl several times. Add the egg and the molasses; beat until blended. Beat in the flour; you might need to stop beating and start stirring the flour in with a spoon as the mixture becomes stiff. In a small bowl, stir together the turbinado sugar and the crystallized ginger. Roll pieces of the cookie dough into 1-inch balls, then roll the balls in the sugar-ginger mixture, coating well. Place the balls on an ungreased cookie sheet, about 2 inches apart. Bake the cookies for 7-10 minutes, until the tops crack and the edges become set and golden brown. Let the cookies cool on the cookie sheet for 1 minute, then remove them to a wire rack to cool completely. Makes approximately 48 cookies, depending on size.

Winter Fruit Crisp

I've loved this rustic dessert ever since Edie introduced the family to it one Thanksgiving a while back. We're not anywhere near fresh cranberry country, but apples are a mainstay in upstate South Carolina farming. Granny Smiths are the choice for this recipe; they hold their shape well during cooking.

We have Edie's friend Barbara Allen to thank for this comfort dish.

3 Granny Smith apples, peeled and sliced
2 cups fresh cranberries
1 (8-ounce) can unsweetened crushed pineapple, with juice
½ cup sugar
1 cup brown sugar
¼ cup all-purpose flour
1 stick butter, softened
1 cup old-fashioned oats (not instant)
1 cup chopped pecans
Ice cream or sweetened whipped cream

Lightly grease a 13x9x2-inch baking pan. Layer the apple slices in the bottom; top with the cranberries, then with the pineapple and its juice. Sprinkle with the ½ cup sugar and let stand while you finish the crisp. In a medium bowl, combine the brown sugar and flour. Use a pastry blender or two knives to cut in the butter until the mixture is crumbly and still has some small lumps of butter visible. Stir in the oats and pecans. Sprinkle over the fruit. Cover and refrigerate for 8 hours. To bake, preheat the oven to 375 degrees. Remove the baking dish from the refrigerator and let the crisp stand at room temperature for 30 minutes. Uncover and bake for 30 minutes. Serve hot or warm with ice cream or whipped cream. Makes 8-10 servings.

Chocolate Mousse Cake

2 dozen lady fingers
¼-½ cup Kahlúa (or other coffee-flavored liqueur)
12 ounces semisweet chocolate
2 (8 ounce) packages cream cheese, softened
½ cup sugar
3 large eggs, separated
2 teaspoons vanilla extract
2 cups whipping cream, whipped
Additional whipped cream, for garnish
Chocolate shavings, for garnish

Line the bottom and sides of a 9-inch springform pan with lady fingers. Sprinkle with Kahlúa. In the top of a double boiler set over simmering water, melt the chocolate. Set aside. In a mixing bowl, beat together the cream cheese and the sugar. Add the egg yolks, one at a time, beating after each addition. Add the melted chocolate and the vanilla; beat until smooth and well-combined. Set aside. Beat the egg whites until stiff peaks form, then fold them into the whipped cream. Fold the chocolate mixture gently into the whipped cream/egg white mixture. Pour on top of the lady fingers in the springform pan. Chill overnight. To serve, remove pan from refrigerator, then remove the sides of the pan. Top with additional whipped cream and some chocolate shavings, if desired. Makes about 10 servings.

Whenever we gather for holidays like Thanksgiving and Christmas, we all share the cooking duties. Come to think of it, though, it's not really a duty – it's a pleasure.

Whenever I get a chance to stake the first claim on what I'd like to contribute, I volunteer to handle the dessert. But I have been known to quickly bow out when Edie has a special new dessert to try.

Edie's friend Leslie Shearin Painter was the first to share this recipe with our family.

You might also want to consider using egg-substitute products that are pasteurized.

This recipe contains uncooked eggs, which can pose a health risk. New "pasteurized-in-the-shell" eggs have gotten a lot of attention as an option for making and enjoying desserts such as this while minimizing any risks. The eggs are heated very slowly and precisely so that they reach the temperature at which disease-causing bacteria are killed.

Date-Nut Snowballs

1½ sticks butter
1 cup sugar
1 (8-ounce) package chopped, pitted dates
2 teaspoons vanilla extract
2 cups crisped rice cereal
1 cup coarsely-chopped pecans
Powdered sugar, for coating balls

The first time I prepared these was in high school, and they made terrific Christmas gifts for my teachers. They're also a nice addition to the spread for a holiday drop-in. I find that even those who turn up their noses at dates will come back for seconds after tasting one of these powdered-sugar-coated treats.

The recipe has made the rounds of many cookbooks, and I don't know the original source.

In a medium-size saucepan over medium to medium-low heat, cook the butter, sugar and dates together for 10 minutes, stirring frequently to keep the mixture from sticking or scorching. Remove the pan from the heat and stir in the vanilla. Place the cereal and the pecan pieces in a large mixing bowl. Pour the date mixture over the cereal and nuts and stir to combine. Let the mixture cool down a little — it should be slightly warm, but cool enough for you to handle. Roll and shape the mixture into balls (about 1-inch size) and place each one on a piece of waxed paper. When the balls have cooled completely, roll each one in powdered sugar to coat. Store in an airtight container. Makes approximately 3 dozen balls, depending on size.

Be sure the date balls have cooled all the way before you roll them in powdered sugar; if they're warm, they tend to soak up the powdered sugar and look like muddy snowballs, rather than freshly-made ones prettily dusted in white.

Piedmont Praline Sauce

1½ cups light corn syrup
½ cup heavy cream
2 tablespoons butter
2 cups pecan halves, lightly toasted
2 teaspoons vanilla extract

In a 2-quart saucepan, stir together the corn syrup, heavy cream and butter until blended. Stirring constantly, bring the mixture to a boil over medium heat; boil for 2 minutes. Remove from the heat and stir in the pecans and the vanilla. Let the sauce cool, then cover and refrigerate it. Serve it hot or cold over ice cream. Store the sauce in a tightly covered container in the refrigerator. To reheat the sauce, cook it over low heat until it's pourable. Makes about 2½ cups.

In the 1960s, '70s and '80s, the "Loved and Lost" recipe column in the Charleston newspaper was required reading for anyone who loved to cook. Charlotte Walker, its author, brought up a whole generation of cooks in the best tradition of the Lowcountry.

This recipe appeared in a 1982 column on Christmas gifts from the kitchen. It's a gooey winner made with fresh pecans.

Betty's Chocolate Cake

This recipe was featured in a newspaper story back in the 1970s. We didn't keep the part (if there was one) that explained who Betty is or was, but we've always called this Betty's Chocolate Cake just the same.

Don't tell folks the cake and frosting contain buttermilk — they might turn it down. It would be their loss, though, because this is a marvelous cake. You don't taste the buttermilk – all you taste is the moistness it gives to every last crumb.

For the cake:

2 cups all-purpose flour
1 teaspoon baking soda
½ teaspoon salt
2 cups granulated sugar
2 sticks butter
4 tablespoons unsweetened cocoa powder
1 cup water
½ cup buttermilk
2 large eggs
1 teaspoon vanilla extract

For the frosting:

1 stick butter
4 tablespoons unsweetened cocoa powder
6 tablespoons buttermilk
1 (16-ounce) box powdered sugar
1 teaspoon vanilla extract
1 cup chopped pecans (optional)

Preheat the oven to 350 degrees. Grease and flour a jelly-roll pan (11x16x1-inch size). To make the cake: combine the flour, baking soda, salt and sugar in a large bowl. In a saucepan, bring the butter, cocoa and water to a boil, then pour the hot mixture over the dry ingredients, whisking to combine. Add the buttermilk, eggs and vanilla; whisk until the batter is smooth (it will be thin). Pour the batter into the pan and bake for 15-20 minutes; the cake is done when it springs back if lightly touched in the center. Place the cake (still in the pan) on a wire rack. Make the frosting immediately after removing the cake from the oven. In a saucepan, bring the butter, cocoa and buttermilk to a boil. Stir in the powdered sugar and vanilla; stir until smooth, making sure no lumps of powdered sugar remain. Stir in the nuts last. Pour the warm frosting carefully over the warm cake, spreading it toward the edges of the pan. Let the frosting set for about 30 minutes, then cut the cake into squares. Makes 24-30 squares.

The Very Big Birthday Cake

2 recipes Betty's Chocolate Cake
1 recipe Betty's Chocolate Cake Frosting

For the cream cheese frosting:

2 (8-ounce) packages cream cheese, softened
2 sticks butter, softened
2 (16-ounce) boxes powdered sugar
2 teaspoons vanilla extract

Line two jelly-roll pans with parchment paper, leaving enough paper hanging over the edges for it to serve as a handle later to lift the cake out of the pan. Prepare two Betty's Chocolate Cakes, baking as directed.

This is a VERY big cake for VERY big birthdays and VERY big groups of people. I stumbled onto it purely by accident.

In January 2001, I was drafted to make the cake for a surprise 50th birthday party for my boss, Steve Mullins. It had to be delicious and it had to be big — more than 50 people were expected at the party. I decided to make two Betty's Chocolate Cakes, but I didn't want to take them to the party in the beat-up old pans that I baked them in. So I lined the pans with parchment paper and left enough paper hanging over the edges to serve as handles. I expected to be able to lift out the cakes and put them on nice-looking serving trays without any problem.

Well, famous last words — one of the cakes broke into a couple of big sections when I was lifting it out of the pan. I had to punt to salvage (and conceal) what I could, and this is what resulted. Not only is it VERY big in all the senses mentioned above, it was a VERY big hit at the party.

Remove from oven and set on racks (still in the pans) to cool. While the cakes cool, prepare the Betty's Chocolate Cake Frosting. Remove one of the cakes from the pan, lifting it out with the parchment paper handles (this will be a whole lot easier if someone is there to help you) and placing it on a large serving plate. Pour the frosting over the cake layer on the plate and spread to the edges (don't worry if a little drips down the sides). Let cool completely.

To make the frosting, cream the cream cheese and butter until smooth and creamy. Beat in the powdered sugar gradually, until smooth. Beat in the vanilla. (You might want to make the frosting in two batches; just divide the ingredients in half – i.e., 1 package cream cheese, 1 stick butter, etc.) To finish the cake, carefully (and with help) place the second Betty's Chocolate Cake layer on top of the first, frosted cake layer. Spread the cream cheese frosting thickly over the top and sides. Makes about 40-50 servings; you can slice it in small squares because it's extremely rich.

Easiest Candied Fruit Cookies

2 sticks butter, softened
1 cup sifted powdered sugar (sift, then measure)
1 large egg
½ teaspoon vanilla extract
2½ cups all-purpose flour
¼ teaspoon salt
¼ teaspoon cream of tartar
¾ cup chopped pecans
½ cup candied pineapple pieces
1¼ cups whole candied cherries, red and green

In a mixing bowl, cream the butter and sugar until light. Beat in the egg and the vanilla. By hand, stir in the flour, salt and cream of tartar until well combined. Stir in the chopped nuts, candied pineapple and whole cherries. Using lightly-floured hands, shape the dough into several logs that are 1½ inches in diameter. Wrap each log tightly in plastic wrap and freeze. When you're ready to bake, preheat the oven to 375 degrees. Lightly spray a cookie sheet with nonstick spray. Slice as many cookies as you need from the rolls of frozen dough; use a wet knife and slice the cookies about ¼-inch thick. Bake the cookies for 6-8 minutes, until just golden in color. Makes 100 cookies (approximately, depending on size).

These are lovely, delicious little holiday cookies that deliver an extra bonus: They're freezer cookies. Just mix the dough, shape it into rolls, wrap the rolls tightly in plastic wrap, and freeze. Then, when people drop by unexpectedly or you find yourself craving just a little bit of something sweet, slice off as many cookies as you need. A quick turn in the oven and they're done!

With the red and green cherries and bits of candied pineapple, they just look like the holiday season.

This recipe makes a lot of cookies – 100 or more, depending on the size of the dough "logs" and how thick you slice the cookies. If wrapped tightly, the dough will keep for at least two months in the freezer.

Benne Cookies

Sesame seeds are popularly known in the Lowcountry as benne seeds. They are one of many, many contributions to local cuisine that were made by blacks brought to the area as slaves.

These benne cookies bake up crisp and sweet. You can prepare the dough and keep it in the freezer for up to two months, slicing and baking as many cookies as you need for a particular occasion, such as unexpected guests or a last-minute gift.

1 cup benne (sesame) seeds
2 cups light brown sugar
1 stick butter, softened
1 egg, lightly beaten
1 teaspoon vanilla extract
1½ cups self-rising flour

Place the benne seeds in a skillet and set it over medium to medium-low heat. Toast the benne seeds until they're golden brown and fragrant; watch them carefully because they can burn easily. Remove them from the heat and let them cool completely. Cream the brown sugar and butter in a mixing bowl until the they're well combined. Add the egg and vanilla and beat to combine. Beat in the flour, then beat or stir in the benne seeds. Using lightly-floured hands, shape the dough into 6 logs, each about 1 inch in diameter. Roll the logs in aluminum foil and freeze at least 6 hours, or overnight. To bake, preheat the oven to 325 degrees. Line cookie sheets with aluminum foil. Remove one log of dough from the freezer, unwrap it, and slice cookies about ¼-inch thick. Place the cookies on the foil, allowing 2 inches between cookies for spreading. Bake for 8-10 minutes in the middle of the oven, until the cookies are rich golden brown. Place the baking sheet on a wire rack and let the cookies cool completely; they can be easily peeled off the foil at that point. Store cookies in an airtight container. Makes 90-100 cookies.

Don't place the unbaked cookies on a warm cookie sheet; they're buttery, so they'll start to melt. Use a cool cookie sheet for each new batch that heads into the oven.

White Christmas Candy

1 (6-ounce) box peppermint candy canes
1 pound good-quality white chocolate, coarsely chopped

Line a cookie sheet with waxed paper. Unwrap the candy canes and place them in a heavy zip-top plastic bag. Using the back of a heavy kitchen spoon, crush the candy until it is broken into small pieces (don't get carried away — the candy shouldn't end up as powder). In the top of a double boiler, melt the white chocolate over low heat, stirring until smooth. Remove the pan immediately from the heat and pour the chocolate on the waxed paper, using a spatula to spread it out smoothly so it's about ⅛-inch thick. Quickly sprinkle the crushed candy canes over the top. Place the cookie sheet, uncovered, in the refrigerator for at least 1 hour, or until the candy is firmly set. Remove the candy from refrigerator and break or cut it into irregularly-shaped pieces. Store in an airtight container. Makes 1 pound of candy.

About five or six years ago we discovered a wonderful candy in a gourmet shop around the holidays. It was creamy white chocolate "bark" studded with pieces of peppermint candy. With its red and white colors, it looked especially pretty for Christmas, but it was also gourmet-candy expensive. This is our less-expensive-but-still-delicious copy.

If you're looking for a wonderful, quick-to-make Christmas gift for a teacher, co-worker, hairdresser or other acquaintance, this is the ticket. Wrap it in a pretty gift bag, tie it with a sparkly ribbon and it's white chocolate cheer in a bag!

If you can find the red-and-green striped candy canes, they add a particularly pretty touch to this treat. Another alternative is to use half red-striped candy canes and half green-striped candy canes, but the green-striped ones can sometimes be hard to find.

Be sure you don't pick up spearmint green candy canes by mistake. Spearmint and white chocolate are not a happy flavor combination! And, as I can tell you from a mistake I made last Christmas, be aware that not all red candy canes are peppermint. Some — as I learned too late — are cherry. Oops.

Index